WHAT'S COOK

vegetarian

Jenny Stacey

p

This is a Parragon Book
This edition published in 2000

Parragon
Queen Street House
4 Queen Street
Bath BA1 1HE, UK

ISBN: 0-75254-418-7 (paperback)
ISBN: 0-75254-406-3 (hardback)

Printed in Indonesia

Produced by Haldane Mason, London

Acknowledgements
Art Director: Ron Samuels
Editorial Director: Sydney Francis
Managing Editor: Jo-Anne Cox
Editorial Assistant: Elizabeth Towers
Design: dap ltd
Photography: Andrew Sydenham
Home Economist: Kathryn Hawkins

Note
Cup measurements in this book are for American cups.
Tablespoons are assumed to be 15 ml. Unless otherwise stated,
milk is assumed to be full fat, eggs are medium
and pepper is freshly ground black pepper.

Contents

Introduction

This book is designed to appeal to vegetarians, demi-vegetarians and vegans alike. Its main aim is to dispel the myth that vegetarian food is brown, stodgy and bland. When browsing through the recipes in this cookbook you will discover just how versatile, colourful and flavourful a vegetarian diet can be.

It makes perfect sense when you consider the wide range of natural produce which is generally available the whole year round. With the advent of refrigerated transport, fresh produce is now brought from all over the world to give us a whole array of fresh fruit and vegetables with which to work. In addition, the use of spices, fresh herbs and garlic, accompanied by sauces and relishes makes for a very exciting and healthy diet.

Eating a balanced, nutritional diet is very important, and can be easily achieved by combining the recipes in this book when planning your meal, to include protein, carbohydrate, vitamins, minerals and some fats. It is very important in any diet, but especially a vegetarian diet, that a good balance is achieved and that sufficient protein is eaten.

The recipes in this book come from far and wide, including the Orient, Middle East and the Mediterranean. There are also more traditional recipes and variations on themes, such as 'vegetable-toad-in-the-hole', a quick, tasty family meal in which it is guaranteed you won't miss the meat. Indeed, this can be said for all of the recipes in this book. Many could be served to meat-eating guests without them missing the 'meat factor' in any way. In fact, this book is the perfect way to introduce your friends to this healthy and delicious diet.

When cooking the following recipes, feel free to substitute some ingredients to suit your specific diets, using soya milk for example in place of cow's milk, cream substitute instead of dairy cream and vegetable margarine in place of butter. You will discover that the vegetarian diet has progressed greatly from the nut cutlet to a colourful and imaginative way of eating. Go ahead and enjoy!

THE VEGETARIAN STORE-CUPBOARD

A well-stocked store-cupboard forms the backbone of any good cook's kitchen, and it is always useful to have plenty of basic foods ready to hand. Use the following information as a checklist when you need to replenish your stocks.

Flour
You will need to keep a selection of flour: plain (all-purpose) and self-raising flour if you want to make your own bread, and wholemeal (whole wheat) flour, either for using on its own or for combining with white flour for cakes and pastries. You may also like to keep some rice flour and cornflour (cornstarch) for thickening sauces and to add to cakes, biscuits and puddings. Buckwheat, chick-pea (garbanzo bean) and soya flours can also be bought. These are useful for pancakes and for combining with other flours to add different flavours and textures.

Grains
A good variety of grains is essential. For rice, choose from long-grain, basmati, Italian arborio for making risotto, short-grain for puddings, and wild rice to add interest. Look out for fragrant Thai rice, jasmine rice and combinations of different varieties to add colour and texture to your dishes. When choosing your rice, remember that brown rice is a better source of vitamin B1 and fibre.

Other grains add variety to the diet. Try to include some barley (whole grain or pearl), millet, bulgur wheat, polenta (made from maize), oats (oatmeal, oatflakes or oatbran), semolina – including cous-cous (from which it is made), sago and tapioca.

Pasta
Pasta is so popular nowadays, and there are many types and shapes to choose from. Keep a good selection, and always make sure you have the basic lasagne sheets, tagliatelle or fettuccine (flat ribbons) and spaghetti. Try spinach- or tomato-flavoured varieties for a change, and sample some of the many fresh pastas now available. Better still, make your own – handrolling pasta, while undoubtedly time-consuming, can be very satisfying, but you can buy a special machine for rolling the dough and cutting certain shapes. You could also buy a wooden 'pasta tree' on which to hang the pasta to dry, in which case you might find you get enthusiastic help especially if you have small children!

Pulses (legumes)

Pulses (legumes) are a valuable source of protein, vitamins and minerals. Stock up on soya beans, haricot (navy) beans, red kidney beans, cannellini beans, chick-peas (garbanzo beans), lentils, split peas and butter beans. Buy dried pulses (legumes) for soaking and cooking yourself, or canned varieties for speed and convenience. Cook dried red and black kidney beans in boiling water for 15 minutes to destroy harmful toxins in the outer skin. Drain and rinse the beans, and then simmer until the beans are tender. Soya beans should be boiled for 1 hour, as they contain a substance that inhibits protein absorption.

Spices and herbs

A good selection of spices and herbs is important for adding variety and interest to your cooking. There are some good spice mixtures available – try Cajun, Chinese five-spice, Indonesian piri-piri and the different curry blends. Try grinding your own spices with a mortar and pestle, or in a coffee mill, to make your own blends, or just experiment with those that you can buy. Although spices will keep well, don't leave them in the cupboard for too long, as they may lose some of their strength. Buy small amounts as you need them.

Fresh herbs are preferable to dried, but it is essential to have dried ones in stock as a useful back-up. Keep the basics such as thyme, rosemary and bay leaves.

Chillies

These come both fresh and dried and in colours from green through yellow, orange and red to brown. The 'hotness' varies so use with caution, but as a guide the smaller they are the hotter they will be. The seeds are hottest and are usually discarded. When cutting chillies with bare hands do not touch your eyes; the juices will cause severe irritation.

Chilli powder should also be used sparingly. Check whether the powder is pure chilli or a chilli seasoning or blend, which should be milder. Chilli sauces are also used widely in oriental cookery, but again they vary in strength from hot to exceedingly hot, as well as in sweetness.

Nuts and seeds

As well as adding protein, vitamins and useful fats to the diet, nuts and seeds add important flavour and texture to vegetarian meals. To bring out the flavour of nuts and seeds, grill (broil) or roast them until lightly browned.

Make sure that you keep a good supply of almonds, brazils, cashews, chestnuts (dried or canned), hazelnuts, peanuts, pecans, pistachios, pine kernels (nuts) and walnuts. Coconut – either creamed or desiccated (shredded) – is useful too.

For your seed collection, have sesame, sunflower, pumpkin and poppy. Pumpkin seeds in particular are a good source of zinc.

Dried fruits

Currants, raisins, sultanas (golden raisins), dates, apples, apricots, figs, pears, peaches, prunes, paw-paws (papayas), mangoes, figs, bananas and pineapples can all be purchased dried and can be used in lots of different recipes. When buying dried fruits, look for untreated varieties: for example, buy figs that have not been rolled in sugar, and choose unsulphured apricots, if they are available.

Oils and fats

Oils are useful for adding subtle flavourings to foods, so it is a good idea to have a selection in your store-cupboard. Use a light olive oil for cooking and extra-virgin olive oil for salad dressings. Use sunflower oil as a good general-purpose oil and select one or two speciality oils to add character to different dishes. Sesame oil is wonderful in stir-fries; hazelnut and walnut oils are superb in salad dressings. Oils and fats add flavour to foods, and contain the important fat-soluble vitamins A, D, E and K. Remember all fats and oils are high in calories, and that oils are higher in calories than butter or margarine – 1 tbsp of oil contains 134 calories, whereas 1 tbsp of butter or margarine contains 110 calories. When you are using oil, it is a good idea to measure it – it's easy to use twice as much without realizing.

Vinegars

Choose three or four vinegars – red or white wine, cider, light malt, tarragon, sherry or balsamic vinegar, to name just a few. Each will add its own character to your recipes.

Mustards

Mustards are made from black, brown or white mustard seeds which are ground, mixed with spices and then, usually, mixed with vinegar. Meaux mustard is made from mixed mustard seeds and has a grainy texture with a warm, spicy taste. Dijon mustard, made from husked and ground mustard seeds, is medium-hot and has a sharp flavour. Its versatility in salads and with barbecues makes it ideal for the vegetarian. German mustard is mild sweet/sour and is best used in Scandinavian and German dishes.

Bottled sauces

Soy sauce is widely used in Eastern cookery and is made from fermented yellow soya beans mixed with wheat, salt, yeast and sugar. Light soy sauce tends to be rather salty, whereas dark soy sauce tends to be sweeter and is more often used in dips and sauces. Teriyaki sauce gives an authentic Japanese flavouring to stir-fries. Thick and dark brown, it contains soy sauce, vinegar, sesame oil and spices as main ingredients. Black bean and yellow bean sauces add an instant authentic Chinese flavour to stir-fries. Black bean sauce is the stronger; the yellow bean variety is milder and is excellent with vegetables.

Soups & Starters

Soup is simple to make but always produces tasty results. There is an enormous variety of soups which you can make with vegetables. They can be rich and creamy, thick and chunky, light and delicate, and hot or chilled. The vegetables are often puréed to give a smooth consistency and thicken the soup, but you can also purée just some of the mixture to give the soup more texture and interest. A wide range of ingredients can be used in addition to vegetables – pulses (legumes), grains, noodles, cheese and yogurt are all good candidates. It is also easy to make substitutions when you don't have certain ingredients to hand.

Starters are an important part of any meal, setting the scene for the remainder of the menu and whetting the appetite. They should therefore be colourful and full of flavour, but balance the remainder of the meal well, not being too filling if a heavier main course is being served, or containing ingredients used in following courses. With this in mind, this chapter is packed with a range of thick and thin flavourful soups for all occasions and a wide range of starters from different origins, be it Oriental, Indian or Mediterranean, they will all make a wonderful start to a meal.

Mixed Bean Soup

This is a really hearty soup, filled with colour, flavour and goodness,
which may be adapted to any vegetables that you have at hand.

Serves 4

INGREDIENTS

1 tbsp vegetable oil
1 red onion, halved and sliced
100 g/3 1/2 oz/2/3 cup potato, diced
1 carrot, diced
1 leek, sliced
1 green chilli, sliced
3 garlic cloves, crushed

1 tsp ground coriander
1 tsp chilli powder
1 litre/1 3/4 pints/4 cups vegetable
   stock
450 g/1 lb mixed canned beans,
   such as red kidney, borlotti,
   black eye or flageolet, drained

salt and pepper
2 tbsp chopped coriander (cilantro),
   to garnish

1 Heat the vegetable oil in a large saucepan and add the prepared onion, potato, carrot and leek. Sauté for about 2 minutes, stirring, until the vegetables are slightly softened.

2 Add the sliced chilli and crushed garlic and cook for a further 1 minute.

3 Stir in the ground coriander, chilli powder and the vegetable stock.

4 Bring the soup to the boil, reduce the heat and cook for 20 minutes or until the vegetables are tender.

5 Stir in the beans, season well with salt and pepper and cook for a further 10 minutes, stirring occasionally.

6 Transfer the soup to a warm tureen or individual bowls, garnish with chopped coriander (cilantro) and serve.

COOK'S TIP

Serve this soup
with slices of warm corn bread
or a cheese loaf.

Vegetable & Corn Chowder

This is a really filling soup, which should be served before a lighter meal.
Packed with corn and fresh vegetables it is easy to prepare and filled with flavour.

Serves 4

INGREDIENTS

1 tbsp vegetable oil
1 red onion, diced
1 red (bell) pepper, diced
3 garlic cloves, crushed
1 large potato, diced
2 tbsp plain (all-purpose) flour

600 ml/1 pint/2^1/$_2$ cups milk
300 ml/^{1}/$_2$ pint/1^1/$_4$ cups vegetable
   stock
50 g/1^3/$_4$ oz broccoli florets
300 g/10^1/$_2$ oz/3 cups canned
   sweetcorn in brine, drained

75 g/2^3/$_4$ oz/^{3}/$_4$ cup vegetarian
   Cheddar cheese, grated
salt and pepper
1 tbsp chopped fresh coriander
   (cilantro), to garnish

1 Heat the oil in a large saucepan and sauté the onion, (bell) pepper, garlic and potato for 2–3 minutes, stirring.

2 Stir in the flour and cook for 30 seconds. Stir in the milk and stock.

3 Add the broccoli and sweetcorn. Bring the mixture to the boil, stirring, then reduce the heat and simmer for about 20 minutes or until the vegetables are tender.

4 Stir in 50 g/1^3/$_4$ oz/^{1}/$_2$ cup of the cheese until it melts.

5 Season and spoon the chowder into a warm soup tureen. Garnish with the remaining cheese and the coriander (cilantro) and serve.

COOK'S TIP

Add a little double (heavy) cream to the soup after adding the milk for a really creamy flavour.

COOK'S TIP

Vegetarian cheeses are made with rennets of non-animal origin, using microbial or fungal enzymes.

Cauliflower & Broccoli Soup with Gruyère

Full of flavour, this creamy cauliflower and broccoli soup is simple to make and delicious to eat.

Serves 4

INGREDIENTS

3 tbsp vegetable oil
1 red onion, chopped
2 garlic cloves, crushed
300 g/10$^{1}/_{2}$ oz cauliflower florets
300 g/10$^{1}/_{2}$ oz broccoli florets
1 tbsp plain (all-purpose) flour

600 ml/1 pint/2$^{1}/_{2}$ cups milk
300 ml/$^{1}/_{2}$ pint/1$^{1}/_{4}$ cups vegetable stock
75 g/2$^{3}/_{4}$ oz/$^{3}/_{4}$ cup vegetarian Gruyère cheese, grated
pinch of paprika

150 ml/$^{1}/_{4}$ pint$^{2}/_{3}$ cup single (light) cream
paprika and vegetarian Gruyère cheese shavings, to garnish

1 Heat the oil in a large saucepan and sauté the onion, garlic, cauliflower and broccoli for 3–4 minutes, stirring constantly. Add the flour and cook for a further 1 minute, stirring.

2 Stir in the milk and stock and bring to the boil. Reduce the heat and simmer for 20 minutes.

3 Remove about a quarter of the vegetables and set aside.

4 Put the remaining soup in a food processor and blend for 30 seconds until smooth. Transfer the soup to a clean saucepan.

5 Return the reserved vegetable pieces to the soup.

6 Stir in the grated cheese, paprika and single (light) cream and heat gently for 2–3 minutes without boiling, or until the cheese starts to melt.

7 Transfer to warm serving bowls, garnish with shavings of Gruyère and dust with paprika.

COOK'S TIP

The soup must not start to boil after the cream has been added otherwise it will curdle. Use natural (unsweetened) yogurt instead of the cream if preferred, but again do not allow to boil.

Celery, Stilton & Walnut Soup

This is a classic combination of ingredients all brought together in a delicious, creamy soup.

Serves 4

INGREDIENTS

50 g/1³/₄ oz/4 tbsp butter
2 shallots, chopped
3 celery sticks, chopped
1 garlic clove, crushed
2 tbsp plain (all-purpose) flour

600 ml/1 pint/2¹/₂ cups vegetable stock
300 ml/¹/₂ pint/1¹/₄ cups milk
150 g/5¹/₂ oz/1¹/₂ cups blue Stilton cheese, crumbled, plus extra to garnish

2 tbsp walnut halves, roughly chopped
150 ml/¹/₄ pint/²/₃ cup natural (unsweetened) yogurt
salt and pepper
chopped celery leaves, to garnish

1 Melt the butter in a large saucepan and sauté the shallots, celery and garlic for 2–3 minutes, stirring, until softened.

2 Add the flour and cook for 30 seconds.

3 Gradually stir in the vegetable stock and milk and bring to the boil.

4 Reduce the heat to a gentle simmer and add the crumbled blue Stilton cheese and walnut halves. Cover and leave to simmer for 20 minutes.

5 Stir in the natural (unsweetened) yogurt and heat for a further 2 minutes without boiling.

6 Season the soup, then transfer to a warm soup tureen or individual serving bowls, garnish with chopped celery leaves and extra crumbled blue Stilton cheese and serve at once.

COOK'S TIP

As well as adding protein, vitamins and useful fats to the diet, nuts add important flavour and texture to vegetarian meals.

VARIATION

Use an alternative blue cheese, such as Dolcelatte or Gorgonzola, if preferred or a strong vegetarian Cheddar cheese, grated.

Curried Parsnip Soup

Parsnips make a delicious soup as they have a slightly sweet flavour. In this recipe, spices are added to complement this sweetness and a dash of lemon juice adds tartness.

Serves 4

INGREDIENTS

1 tbsp vegetable oil
1 tbsp butter
1 red onion, chopped
3 parsnips, chopped
2 garlic cloves, crushed

2 tsp garam masala
$^1/_2$ tsp chilli powder
1 tbsp plain (all-purpose) flour
850 ml/1$^1/_2$ pints/3$^3/_4$ cups vegetable stock

grated rind and juice of 1 lemon
salt and pepper
lemon zest, to garnish

1 Heat the oil and butter in a large saucepan until the butter has melted.

2 Add the onion, parsnips and garlic and sauté for 5–7 minutes, stirring, until the vegetables have softened.

3 Add the garam masala and chilli powder and cook for 30 seconds, stirring well.

4 Sprinkle in the flour, mixing well and cook for a further 30 seconds.

5 Stir in the stock, lemon rind and juice and bring to the boil. Reduce the heat and simmer for 20 minutes.

6 Remove some of the vegetable pieces with a slotted spoon and reserve until required. Blend the remaining soup and vegetables in a food processor for 1 minute or until smooth.

7 Return the soup to a clean saucepan and stir in the reserved vegetables. Heat the soup through for 2 minutes.

8 Season then transfer to soup bowls, garnish with grated lemon zest and serve.

VARIATION

Use 1 medium orange instead of the lemon if preferred and garnish with grated orange zest.

Jerusalem Artichoke Soup

Jerusalem artichokes belong to the tuber family. They are native to North America, but are also grown in Europe. They have a delicious nutty flavour which combines well with orange.

Serves 4

INGREDIENTS

675 g/1¹/₂ lb Jerusalem artichokes
5 tbsp orange juice
25 g/1 oz/2 tbsp butter
1 leek, chopped

1 garlic clove, crushed
300 ml/¹/₂ pint/1¹/₄ cups vegetable
  stock
150 ml/¹/₄ pint/²/₃ cup milk

2 tbsp chopped coriander (cilantro)
150 ml/¹/₄ pint/²/₃ cup natural
  (unsweetened) yogurt
grated orange rind, to garnish

1 Rinse the Jerusalem artichokes and place in a large saucepan with 2 tablespoons of the orange juice and enough water to cover. Bring to the boil, reduce the heat and cook for 20 minutes or until the artichokes are tender.

2 Drain the artichokes, reserving 425 ml/³/₄ pint/ 2 cups of the cooking liquid. Leave the artichokes to cool.

3 Once cooled, peel the artichokes and place in a large bowl. Mash the flesh with a potato masher.

4 Melt the butter in a large saucepan and sauté the leek and garlic for 2–3 minutes, stirring until the leek softens.

5 Stir in the artichoke flesh, the reserved cooking water, the stock, milk and remaining orange juice. Bring the soup to the boil, reduce the heat and simmer for 2–3 minutes.

6 Remove a few pieces of leek with a slotted spoon and reserve. Transfer the remainder of the soup to a food processor and blend for 1 minute until smooth.

7 Return the soup to a clean saucepan and stir in the reserved leeks, coriander (cilantro) and yogurt.

8 Transfer to individual soup bowls, garnish with orange rind and serve.

VARIATION

If Jerusalem artichokes are unavailable, you could use sweet potatoes instead.

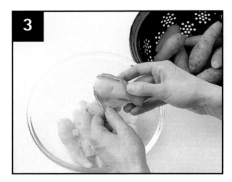

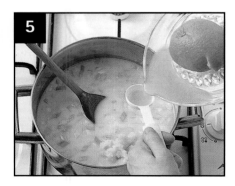

Red (Bell) Pepper & Chilli Soup

This soup has a real Mediterranean flavour, using sweet red (bell) peppers, tomato, chilli and basil. It is great served with a warm olive bread.

Serves 4

INGREDIENTS

225 g/8 oz red (bell) peppers, seeded and sliced
1 onion, sliced
2 garlic cloves, crushed
1 green chilli, chopped

300 ml/^{1}/$_2$ pint/1^1/$_2$ cups passata (sieved tomatoes)
600 ml/1 pint/2^1/$_2$ cups vegetable stock

2 tbsp chopped basil
fresh basil sprigs, to garnish

1 Put the (bell) peppers in a large saucepan with the onion, garlic and chilli. Add the passata (sieved tomatoes) and vegetable stock and bring to the boil, stirring well.

2 Reduce the heat to a simmer and cook for 20 minutes or until the (bell) peppers have softened. Drain, reserving the liquid and vegetables separately.

3 Sieve the vegetables by pressing through a sieve (strainer) with the back of a spoon. Alternatively, blend in a food processor until smooth.

4 Return the vegetable purée to a clean saucepan with the reserved cooking liquid. Add the basil and heat through until hot. Garnish the soup with fresh basil sprigs and serve.

COOK'S TIP

Basil is a useful herb to grow at home. It can be grown easily in a window box.

VARIATION

This soup is also delicious served cold with 150 ml/^{1}/$_4$ pint/ ^{2}/$_3$ cup of natural (unsweetened) yogurt swirled into it.

Dahl Soup

*Dahl is the name given to a delicious Indian lentil dish. This soup is a variation of the theme –
it is made with red lentils and spiced with curry powder.*

Serves 4

INGREDIENTS

25 g/1 oz/2 tbsp butter
2 garlic cloves, crushed
1 onion, chopped
$1/2$ tsp turmeric
1 tsp garam masala
$1/4$ tsp chilli powder
1 tsp ground cumin

1 kg/2 lb 4 oz canned, chopped
  tomatoes, drained
175 g/6 oz/1 cup red lentils
2 tsp lemon juice
600 ml/1 pint/$2^{1}/2$ cups vegetable
  stock

300 ml/$^{1}/2$ pint/$1^{1}/4$ cups coconut
  milk
salt and pepper
chopped coriander (cilantro) and
  lemon slices, to garnish
naan bread, to serve

1 Melt the butter in a large
saucepan and sauté the garlic
and onion for 2–3 minutes,
stirring. Add the spices and cook
for a further 30 seconds.

2 Stir in the tomatoes, red
lentils, lemon juice, vegetable
stock and coconut milk and bring
to the boil.

3 Reduce the heat and simmer
for 25–30 minutes until the
lentils are tender and cooked.

4 Season to taste and spoon
the soup into a warm tureen.
Garnish and serve with warm
naan bread.

COOK'S TIP

*You can buy cans of coconut milk
from supermarkets and
delicatessens. It can also be made by
grating creamed coconut, which
comes in the form of a solid bar, and
mixing it with water.*

COOK'S TIP

*Add small quantities
of hot water to the pan
whilst the lentils are
cooking if they begin to
absorb too much of the liquid.*

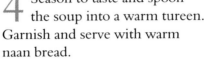

Avocado & Vegetable Soup

Avocado has a rich flavour and colour which makes a creamy flavoured soup.
It is best served chilled, but may be eaten warm as well.

Serves 4

INGREDIENTS

1 large, ripe avocado

2 tbsp lemon juice

1 tbsp vegetable oil

50 g/1^3/4 oz/^{1}/2 cup canned
   sweetcorn, drained

2 tomatoes, peeled and seeded

1 garlic clove, crushed

1 leek, chopped

1 red chilli, chopped

425 ml/^{3}/4 pint/2 cups vegetable
   stock

150 ml/^{1}/4 pint/^{2}/3 cup milk

shredded leeks, to garnish

1 Peel and mash the avocado with a fork, stir in the lemon juice and reserve until required.

2 Heat the oil in a pan and sauté the sweetcorn, tomatoes, garlic, leek and chilli for 2–3 minutes or until the vegetables are softened.

3 Put half of the vegetable mixture in a food processor or blender with the avocado and blend until smooth. Transfer to a clean saucepan.

4 Add the stock, milk and reserved vegetables and cook gently for 3–4 minutes until hot. Garnish and serve.

COOK'S TIP

To remove the stone from an avocado, first cut the avocado in half, then holding one half in your hand, rap the stone with a knife until it is embedded in the stone, then twist the knife until the stone is dislodged.

COOK'S TIP

If serving chilled, transfer from the food processor to a bowl, stir in the stock and milk, cover and chill in the refrigerator for at least 4 hours.

Spanish Tomato Soup with Garlic Bread Croûtons

This Mediterranean tomato soup is thickened with bread,
as is traditional in some parts of Spain.

Serves 4

INGREDIENTS

4 tbsp olive oil
1 onion, chopped
3 garlic cloves, crushed
1 green (bell) pepper, chopped
$^1/_2$ tsp chilli powder
450 g/1 lb tomatoes, chopped
225 g/8 oz French or
   Italian bread, cubed

1 litre/1$^3/_4$ pints/4 cups vegetable
   stock

GARLIC BREAD:
4 slices ciabatta or French bread
4 tbsp olive oil
2 garlic cloves, crushed
25 g/1 oz/$^1/_4$ cup grated
   vegetarian Cheddar
chilli powder, to garnish

1 Heat the olive oil in a large frying pan (skillet) and add the prepared onion, garlic and (bell) pepper. Sauté the vegetables for 2–3 minutes or until the onion has softened.

2 Add the chilli powder and tomatoes and cook over a medium heat until the mixture has thickened.

3 Stir in the bread cubes and stock and cook for 10–15 minutes until the soup is thick and fairly smooth.

4 To make the garlic bread, toast the bread slices under a medium grill (broiler). Drizzle the oil over the top of the bread, rub with the garlic, sprinkle with the cheese and return to the grill (broiler) for 2–3 minutes until the cheese has melted. Sprinkle with chilli powder and serve with the soup.

VARIATION

Replace the green (bell) pepper
with red (bell) pepper,
if you prefer.

Broad (Fava) Bean & Mint Soup

Fresh broad (fava) beans are best for this recipe, but if they are unavailable, use frozen beans instead. They combine well with the fresh flavour of mint.

Serves 4

INGREDIENTS

2 tbsp olive oil
1 red onion, chopped
2 garlic cloves, crushed
2 potatoes, diced
450 g/1 lb/3 cups broad (fava) beans,
  thawed if frozen

850 ml/1¹/₂ pints/3³/₄ cups vegetable
  stock
2 tbsp freshly chopped mint
fresh mint sprigs and yogurt,
  to garnish

1 Heat the olive oil in a large saucepan and sauté the onion and garlic for 2–3 minutes until softened.

2 Add the potatoes and cook for 5 minutes, stirring well.

3 Stir in the beans and the stock, cover and simmer for 30 minutes or until the beans and potatoes are tender.

4 Remove a few vegetables with a slotted spoon and set aside until required. Place the remainder of the soup in a food processor or blender and purée until smooth.

5 Return the soup to a clean saucepan and add the reserved vegetables and mint. Stir well and heat through gently.

6 Transfer the soup to a warm tureen or individual serving bowls. Garnish with swirls of yogurt and sprigs of fresh mint and serve immediately.

VARIATION

Use fresh coriander (cilantro) and ¹/₂ tsp ground cumin as flavourings in the soup, if you prefer.

Crispy Potato Skins

Potato skins are always a favourite. Prepare the skins in advance and warm through before serving with the salad fillings.

Serves 4

INGREDIENTS

4 large baking potatoes
2 tbsp vegetable oil
4 tsp salt
150 ml/¹/₄ pint/²/₃ cup soured cream
   and 2 tbsp chopped chives, to serve
snipped chives, to garnish

BEAN SPROUT SALAD:
50 g/1³/₄ oz/¹/₂ cup bean sprouts
1 celery stick, sliced
1 orange, peeled and segmented
1 red dessert (eating) apple, chopped
¹/₂ red (bell) pepper, chopped
1 tbsp chopped parsley
1 tbsp light soy sauce
1 tbsp clear honey
1 small garlic clove, crushed

BEAN FILLING:
100 g/3¹/₂ oz/1¹/₂ cups canned,
   mixed beans, drained
1 onion, halved and sliced
1 tomato, chopped
2 spring onions (scallions), chopped
2 tsp lemon juice
salt and pepper

1 Scrub the potatoes and put on a baking tray (cookie sheet). Prick the potatoes all over with a fork and rub the oil and salt into the skin.

2 Cook in a preheated oven at 200°C/400°F/Gas Mark 6 for 1 hour or until soft.

3 Cut the potatoes in half lengthwise and scoop out the flesh, leaving a 1 cm/¹/₂ inch thick shell. Put the shells, skin side uppermost, in the oven for 10 minutes until crisp.

4 Mix the ingredients for the bean sprout salad in a bowl, tossing in the soy sauce, honey and garlic to coat.

5 Mix the ingredients for the bean filling in a separate bowl.

6 Mix the soured cream and chives in another bowl.

7 Serve the potato skins hot, with the two salad fillings, garnished with snipped chives, and the sour cream and chive sauce.

Tomato, Olive & Mozzarella Bruschetta

*These simple toasts are filled with colour and flavour. They are great
as a speedy starter or delicious as an appetiser with a good red wine.*

Serves 4

INGREDIENTS

4 muffins
4 garlic cloves, crushed
2 tbsp butter
1 tbsp chopped basil
4 large, ripe tomatoes
1 tbsp tomato purée (paste)

8 pitted black olives, halved
50 g/1³/₄ oz Mozzarella
 cheese, sliced
salt and pepper
fresh basil leaves, to garnish

DRESSING:
1 tbsp olive oil
2 tsp lemon juice
1 tsp clear honey

1 Cut the muffins in half to give eight thick pieces. Toast the muffin halves under a hot grill (broiler) for 2–3 minutes until golden.

2 Mix the garlic, butter and basil together and spread on to each muffin half.

3 Cut a cross shape at the base of each tomato. Plunge the tomatoes in a bowl of boiling water – this will make the skin easier to peel. After a few minutes, pick each tomato up with a fork and peel away the skin. Chop the tomato flesh and mix with the tomato purée (paste) and olives. Divide the mixture between the muffins.

4 Mix the dressing ingredients and drizzle over each muffin. Arrange the Mozzarella cheese on top and season.

5 Return the muffins to the grill (broiler) for 1–2 minutes until the cheese melts.

6 Garnish with fresh basil leaves and serve at once.

VARIATION

Use balsamic vinegar instead of the lemon juice for an authentic Mediterranean flavour.

Lentil Pâté

Red lentils are used in this spicy recipe for speed as they do not require pre-soaking.
If you have other lentils, soak and pre-cook them and use instead of the red lentils.

Serves 4

INGREDIENTS

1 tbsp vegetable oil, plus extra for
  greasing
1 onion, chopped
2 garlic cloves, crushed
1 tsp garam masala

^{1}/$_2$ tsp ground coriander
850 ml/1^1/$_2$ pints/1^1/$_4$ cups vegetable
  stock
175 g/6 oz/^{3}/$_4$ cup red lentils
1 small egg

2 tbsp milk
2 tbsp mango chutney
2 tbsp chopped parsley
chopped parsley, to garnish
salad leaves and warm toast, to serve

1 Heat the oil in a large saucepan and sauté the onion and garlic for 2–3 minutes, stirring. Add the spices and cook for a further 30 seconds.

2 Stir in the stock and lentils and bring the mixture to the boil. Reduce the heat and simmer for 20 minutes until the lentils are cooked and softened. Remove the pan from the heat and drain off any excess moisture.

3 Put the mixture in a food processor and add the egg, milk, mango chutney and parsley. Blend until smooth.

4 Grease and line the base of a 450 g/1 lb loaf tin (pan) and spoon the mixture into the tin (pan), levelling the surface. Cover and cook in a preheated oven at 200°C/400°F/Gas Mark 6 for 40–45 minutes or until firm to the touch.

5 Allow the pâté to cool in the tin (pan) for 20 minutes, then transfer to the refrigerator to cool completely.

6 Turn out the pâté on to a serving plate, slice and garnish with chopped parsley. Serve with salad leaves and warm toast.

VARIATION

Use other spices, such as chilli powder or Chinese five-spice powder, to flavour the pâté and add tomato relish or chilli relish instead of the mango chutney, if you prefer.

Roasted Vegetables on Muffins

*Roasted vegetables are delicious and attractive. Served on warm muffins
with a herb sauce, they are unbeatable.*

Serves 4

INGREDIENTS

1 red onion, cut into eight
1 aubergine (eggplant),
    halved and sliced
1 yellow (bell) pepper, sliced
1 courgette (zucchini), sliced
4 tbsp olive oil
1 tbsp garlic vinegar
2 tbsp vermouth

2 garlic cloves, crushed
1 tbsp chopped thyme
2 tsp light brown sugar
4 muffins, halved
salt and pepper

SAUCE:
2 tbsp butter
1 tbsp flour
150 ml/$^1/_4$ pint/$^2/_3$ cup milk
85 ml/3 fl oz vegetable stock
75 g/2$^3/_4$ oz/$^3/_4$ cup vegetarian
    Cheddar, grated
1 tsp wholegrain mustard
3 tbsp chopped mixed herbs

1 Arrange the vegetables in a
shallow ovenproof dish.
Mix together the oil, vinegar,
vermouth, garlic, thyme and sugar
and pour over the vegetables.
Leave to marinate for 1 hour.

2 Transfer the vegetables to a
baking tray (cookie sheet).
Cook in a pre-heated oven at
200°C/400°F/Gas Mark 6 for
20–25 minutes or until the
vegetables have softened.

3 Meanwhile, make the sauce.
Melt the butter in a small pan
and add the flour. Cook for 1
minute and remove from the heat.
Stir in the milk and stock and
return the pan to the heat. Bring to
the boil, stirring, until thickened.
Stir in the cheese, mustard and
mixed herbs and season well.

4 Preheat the grill (broiler) to
high. Cut the muffins in half
and grill for 2–3 minutes until

golden brown, then remove and
arrange on a serving plate.

5 Spoon the roasted vegetables
on to the muffins and
pour the sauce over the top.
Serve immediately.

Hummus & Garlic Toasts

Hummus is a real favourite spread on these garlic toasts for a delicious starter or as part of a light lunch.

Serves 4

INGREDIENTS

HUMMUS:
400 g/14 oz can chick-peas
   (garbanzo beans)
juice of 1 large lemon
6 tbsp tahini (sesame seed paste)
2 tbsp olive oil

2 garlic cloves, crushed
salt and pepper
chopped fresh coriander (cilantro)
   and black olives, to garnish

TOASTS:
1 ciabatta loaf, sliced
2 garlic cloves, crushed
1 tbsp chopped fresh coriander
   (cilantro)
4 tbsp olive oil

1 To make the hummus, firstly drain the chick-peas (garbanzo beans), reserving a little of the liquid. Put the chick-peas (garbanzo beans) and liquid in a food processor and blend, gradually adding the reserved liquid and lemon juice. Blend well after each addition until smooth.

2 Stir in the tahini (sesame seed paste) and all but 1 teaspoon of the olive oil. Add the garlic, season to taste and blend again until smooth.

3 Spoon the hummus into a serving dish. Drizzle the remaining olive oil over the top, garnish with chopped coriander (cilantro) and olives. Leave to chill in the refrigerator whilst preparing the toasts.

4 Lay the slices of ciabatta on a grill (broiler) rack in a single layer.

5 Mix the garlic, coriander (cilantro) and olive oil together and drizzle over the bread slices. Cook under a hot grill (broiler) for 2–3 minutes until golden brown, turning once. Serve hot with the hummus.

COOK'S TIP

Make the hummus 1 day in advance, and chill, covered, in the refrigerator until required. Garnish and serve.

Mixed Bean Pâté

This is a really quick starter to prepare if canned beans are used.
Choose a wide variety of beans for colour and flavour or use a can of mixed beans.

Serves 4

INGREDIENTS

400 g/14 oz can mixed beans,
  drained
2 tbsp olive oil
juice of 1 lemon
2 garlic cloves, crushed

1 tbsp chopped fresh coriander
  (cilantro)
2 spring onions (scallions), chopped
salt and pepper

shredded spring onions (scallions),
  to garnish

1 Rinse the beans thoroughly under cold running water and drain well.

2 Transfer the beans to a food processor or blender and process until smooth. Alternatively, place the beans in a bowl and mash with a fork or potato masher.

3 Add the olive oil, lemon juice, garlic, coriander (cilantro) and spring onions (scallions) and blend until fairly smooth. Season with salt and pepper to taste.

4 Transfer the pâté to a serving bowl and chill for at least 30 minutes. Garnish with shredded spring onions (scallions) and serve.

COOK'S TIP

Use canned beans which have no salt or sugar added and always rinse thoroughly before use.

COOK'S TIP

Serve the pâté with warm pitta bread or granary toast.

Vegetable Fritters with Sweet & Sour Sauce

These mixed vegetable fritters are coated in a light batter and deep fried until golden for a deliciously crisp coating. They are ideal with the sweet and sour dipping sauce.

Serves 4

INGREDIENTS

100 g/3^1/$_2$ oz/^{3}/$_4$ cup wholemeal
   (whole wheat) flour
pinch of salt
pinch of cayenne pepper
4 tsp olive oil
12 tbsp cold water
100 g/3^1/$_2$ oz broccoli florets
100 g/3^1/$_2$ oz cauliflower florets
50 g/1^3/$_4$ oz mangetout (snow peas)

1 large carrot, cut into batons
1 red (bell) pepper, sliced
2 egg whites, beaten
oil, for deep-frying

SAUCE:
150 ml/^{1}/$_4$ pint/^{2}/$_3$ cup pineapple
   juice
150 ml/^{1}/$_4$ pint/^{2}/$_3$ cup vegetable
   stock
2 tbsp wine vinegar
2 tbsp light brown sugar
2 tsp cornflour (cornstarch)
2 spring onions (scallions), chopped

1 Sieve the flour and salt into a mixing bowl and add the cayenne pepper. Make a well in the centre and gradually beat in the oil and cold water to make a smooth batter.

2 Cook the vegetables in boiling water for 5 minutes and drain well.

3 Whisk the egg whites until peaking and fold them into the flour batter.

4 Dip the vegetables into the batter, turning to coat well. Drain off any excess batter. Heat the oil for deep-frying in a deep fat fryer to 180°C/350°F or until a cube of bread browns in

30 seconds. Fry the vegetables for 1–2 minutes, in batches, until golden. Remove from the oil with a slotted spoon and drain on paper towels.

5 Place all of the sauce ingredients in a pan and bring to the boil, stirring, until thickened and clear. Serve with the fritters.

Mixed Bhajis

These small bhajis are served in Indian restaurants as accompaniments to a main meal, but they are delicious as a starter with a small salad and yogurt sauce.

Serves 4

INGREDIENTS

BAHJIS:
175 g/6 oz/1^1/4 cups gram flour
1 tsp bicarbonate of soda
2 tsp ground coriander
1 tsp garam masala
1^1/2 tsp turmeric
1^1/2 tsp chilli powder

2 tbsp chopped coriander (cilantro)
1 small onion, halved and sliced
1 small leek, sliced
100 g/3^1/2 oz cooked cauliflower
9-12 tbsp cold water
salt and pepper
vegetable oil, for deep-frying

SAUCE:
150 ml/^{1}/4 pint/^{2}/3 cup natural
   (unsweetened) yogurt
2 tbsp chopped mint
^{1}/2 tsp turmeric
1 garlic clove, crushed
fresh mint sprigs, to garnish

1 Sieve the flour, bicarbonate of soda and salt to taste into a mixing bowl and add the spices and fresh coriander (cilantro). Mix well until the ingredients are thoroughly combined.

2 Divide the mixture into 3 and place in separate bowls. Stir the onion into one bowl, the leek into another and the cauliflower into the third bowl. Add 3–4 tbsp of water to each bowl and mix each to form a smooth paste.

3 Heat the oil for deep frying in a deep fat fryer to 180°C/350°F or until a cube of bread browns in 30 seconds. Using 2 dessert spoons, form the mixture into rounds and cook each in the oil for 3–4 minutes until browned. Remove with a slotted spoon and drain on absorbent paper towels. Keep the bhajis warm in the oven whilst cooking the remainder.

4 Mix all of the sauce ingredients together and pour into a serving bowl. Garnish with mint sprigs and serve with the warm bhajis.

VARIATION

If you prefer, use cooked broccoli instead of the cauliflower or cooked, drained spinach instead of the leek for a range of different flavoured bhajis.

Mushroom & Garlic Soufflés

These individual soufflés are very impressive starters, but must be cooked just before serving to prevent them sinking.

Serves 4

INGREDIENTS

50 g/1³/₄ oz/4 tbsp butter
75 g/2³/₄ oz/1 cup flat mushrooms, chopped
2 tsp lime juice

2 garlic cloves, crushed
2 tbsp chopped marjoram
25 g/1 oz/3 tbsp plain (all-purpose) flour

225 ml/8 fl oz/1 cup milk
salt and pepper
2 eggs, separated

1 Lightly grease the inside of four 150 ml/¼ pint individual soufflé dishes with a little butter.

2 Melt 25 g/1 oz/2 tbsp of the butter in a frying pan (skillet). Add the mushrooms, lime juice and garlic and sauté for 2–3 minutes. Remove the mushroom mixture from the frying pan (skillet) with a slotted spoon and transfer to a mixing bowl. Stir in the marjoram.

3 Melt the remaining butter in a pan. Add the flour and cook for 1 minute, then remove from the heat. Stir in the milk and return to the heat. Bring to the boil, stirring until thickened.

4 Add the sauce to the mushroom mixture, mixing well and beat in the egg yolks.

5 Whisk the egg whites until peaking and fold into the mushroom mixture until fully incorporated.

6 Divide the mixture between the soufflé dishes. Place the dishes on a baking tray (cookie sheet) and cook in a preheated oven, 200°C/400°F/Gas Mark 6, for 8–10 minutes or until the soufflés have risen and are cooked through. Serve immediately.

COOK'S TIP

Insert a skewer into the centre of the soufflés to test if they are cooked through – it should come out clean. If not, cook for a few minutes longer, but do not overcook otherwise they will become rubbery.

Carrot, Fennel & Potato Medley

*This is a colourful dish of shredded vegetables in a fresh garlic and honey dressing.
It is delicious served with crusty bread to mop up the dressing.*

Serves 4

INGREDIENTS

2 tbsp olive oil
1 potato, cut into thin strips
1 fennel bulb, cut into thin strips
2 carrots, grated
1 red onion, cut into thin strips
chopped chives and fennel fronds, to
　garnish

DRESSING:
3 tbsp olive oil
1 tbsp garlic wine vinegar
1 garlic clove, crushed
1 tsp Dijon mustard
2 tsp clear honey
salt and pepper

1 Heat the olive oil in a frying pan (skillet), add the potato and fennel slices and cook for 2–3 minutes until beginning to brown. Remove from the frying pan (skillet) with a slotted spoon and drain on paper towels.

2 Arrange the carrot, red onion, potato and fennel in separate piles on a serving platter.

3 Mix the dressing ingredients together and pour over the vegetables. Toss well and sprinkle with chopped chives and fennel fronds. Serve immediately or leave in the refrigerator until required.

VARIATION

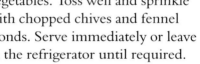

Use mixed, grilled (bell) peppers or shredded leeks in this dish for variety, or add bean sprouts and a segmented orange, if you prefer.

COOK'S TIP

Fennel is an aromatic plant which has a delicate, aniseed flavour. It can be eaten raw in salads, or boiled, braised, sautéed or grilled (broiled). For this salad, if fennel is unavailable, substitute 350 g/ 12 oz sliced leeks.

Onions à la Grecque

This is a well-known method of cooking vegetables and is perfect with shallots or onions, served with a crisp salad.

Serves 4

INGREDIENTS

450 g/1 lb shallots
3 tbsp olive oil
3 tbsp clear honey
2 tbsp garlic wine vinegar
3 tbsp dry white wine
1 tbsp tomato purée (paste)

2 celery stalks, sliced
2 tomatoes, seeded and chopped
salt and pepper
chopped celery leaves, to garnish

1 Peel the shallots. Heat the oil in a large saucepan, add the shallots and cook, stirring, for 3–5 minutes or until they begin to brown.

2 Add the honey and cook for a further 30 seconds over a high heat, then add the garlic wine vinegar and dry white wine, stirring well.

3 Stir in the tomato purée (paste), celery and tomatoes and bring the mixture to the boil.

Cook over a high heat for 5–6 minutes. Season to taste and leave to cool slightly.

4 Garnish with chopped celery leaves and serve warm or cold from the refrigerator.

COOK'S TIP

This dish, served warm, would also make an ideal accompaniment to Chick-pea (Garbanzo Bean) Roast (page 114).

VARIATION

Use button mushrooms instead of the shallots and fennel instead of the celery for another great starter.

Aubergine (Eggplant) Timbale

This is a great way to serve pasta as a starter, wrapped in an aubergine (eggplant) mould (mold). It looks really impressive yet it is so easy to make.

Serves 4

INGREDIENTS

1 large aubergine (eggplant)
50 g/1³/4 oz/¹/2 cup macaroni
1 tbsp vegetable oil
1 onion, chopped
2 garlic cloves, crushed
2 tbsp drained canned sweetcorn
2 tbsp frozen peas, thawed
100 g/3¹/2 oz spinach

25 g/1 oz/¹/4 cup vegetarian Cheddar, grated
1 egg, beaten
225 g/8 oz/3 cups canned, chopped tomatoes
1 tbsp chopped basil
salt and pepper

SAUCE:
4 tbsp olive oil
2 tbsp white wine vinegar
2 garlic cloves, crushed
3 tbsp chopped basil
1 tbsp caster (superfine) sugar

1 Cut the aubergine (eggplant) lengthwise into thin strips, using a potato peeler. Place in a bowl of salted boiling water and leave to stand for 3–4 minutes. Drain well.

2 Lightly grease four 150 ml/ ¼ pint individual ramekin dishes and use the aubergine (eggplant) slices to line the dishes, leaving 2.5 cm/1 inch of aubergine (eggplant) overlapping.

3 Cook the pasta in a pan of boiling water for 8–10 minutes until 'al dente'. Drain. Heat the oil in a pan and sauté the onion and garlic for 2–3 minutes. Stir in the sweetcorn and peas and remove from the heat.

4 Blanch the spinach, drain well, chop and reserve. Add the pasta to the onion mixture with the cheese, egg, tomatoes and basil. Season and mix. Half-fill

each ramekin with some of the pasta. Spoon the spinach on top and then the remaining pasta mixture. Fold the aubergine (eggplant) over the pasta filling to cover. Put the ramekins in a roasting tin (pan) half-filled with boiling water, cover and cook in a preheated oven, 180°C/350°F/Gas Mark 4, for 20–25 minutes or until set. Meanwhile, heat the sauce ingredients in a pan. Turn out the ramekins and serve with the sauce.

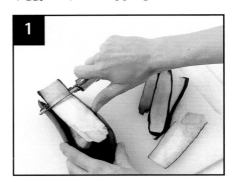

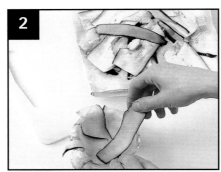

Snacks & Light Meals

The ability to rustle up a simple snack or a quickly-prepared light meal can be very important in our busy lives. Sometimes we may not feel like eating a full-scale meal but nevertheless want something appetizing and satisfying. Or if lunch or dinner is going to be served very late, then we may want something to tide us over. Whether it is for a sustaining snack to break the day, or hearty nibbles to serve with pre-dinner drinks or as a starter, or an informal lunch or supper party, you'll find a mouthwatering collection of recipes in this chapter. They cater for all tastes and times of day, and many can be prepared ahead of time and will not detain you in the kitchen for too long.

There are many easy-to-prepare dishes in this chapter which will satisfy your hunger as well as your taste-buds, with hardly a sandwich in sight! You will easily find something to sustain you which is lighter than the main meal dishes in the following chapter, but may also be served with an accompaniment or crisp salad, a selection of which you will find later in the book.

Garlic Mushrooms on Toast

This is so simple to prepare and looks great if you use a variety of mushrooms for shape and texture. Cooked in garlic butter, they are simply irresistible.

Serves 4

INGREDIENTS

75 g/2³/4 oz/6 tbsp vegetarian
  margarine
2 garlic cloves, crushed

350 g/12 oz/4 cups mixed
  mushrooms, such as open-cap,
  button, oyster and shiitake, sliced
8 slices French bread
1 tbsp chopped parsley

salt and pepper

1 Melt the margarine in a frying pan (skillet). Add the crushed garlic and cook for 30 seconds, stirring.

2 Add the mushrooms and cook for 5 minutes, turning occasionally.

3 Toast the French bread slices under a preheated medium grill (broiler) for 2–3 minutes, turning once.

4 Transfer the toasts to a serving plate.

5 Toss the parsley into the mushrooms, mixing well, and season well with salt and pepper to taste.

6 Spoon the mushroom mixture over the bread and serve immediately.

COOK'S TIP

Add seasonings, such as curry powder or chilli powder, to the mushrooms for extra flavour, if liked.

COOK'S TIP

Store mushrooms for 24–36 hours in the refrigerator, in paper bags, as they sweat in plastic. Wild mushrooms should be washed but other varieties can simply be wiped with paper towels.

Potato, (Bell) Pepper & Mushroom Hash

This is a quick one-pan dish which is ideal for a quick snack. Packed with colour and flavour it is very versatile and you can add any other vegetable you have at hand.

Serves 4

INGREDIENTS

675 g/1¹/₂ lb potatoes, cubed
1 tbsp olive oil
2 garlic cloves, crushed
1 green (bell) pepper, cubed
1 yellow (bell) pepper, cubed

3 tomatoes, diced
75 g/2³/₄ oz/1 cup button
  mushrooms, halved
1 tbsp vegetarian Worcester sauce
2 tbsp chopped basil

salt and pepper
fresh basil sprigs, to garnish
warm, crusty bread, to serve

1 Cook the potatoes in a saucepan of boiling salted water for 7–8 minutes. Drain well and reserve.

2 Heat the oil in a large, heavy-based frying pan (skillet) and cook the potatoes for 8–10 minutes, stirring until browned.

3 Add the garlic and (bell) peppers and cook for 2–3 minutes.

4 Stir in the tomatoes and mushrooms and cook, stirring, for 5–6 minutes.

5 Stir in the vegetarian Worcester sauce and basil and season well. Garnish and serve with crusty bread.

VARIATION

This dish can also be eaten cold as a salad.

COOK'S TIP

Most brands of Worcester sauce contain anchovies so make sure you choose a vegetarian variety.

Vegetable Samosas

These Indian snacks are perfect for a quick or light meal.
Served with a salad they can be made in advance and frozen for ease.

Makes 12

INGREDIENTS

FILLING:
2 tbsp vegetable oil
1 onion, chopped
$^1/_2$ tsp ground coriander
$^1/_2$ tsp ground cumin
pinch of turmeric

$^1/_2$ tsp ground ginger
$^1/_2$ tsp garam masala
1 garlic clove, crushed
225 g/8 oz/1$^1/_2$ cups potatoes, diced
100 g/3$^1/_2$ oz/1 cup frozen peas, thawed

150 g/5$^1/_2$ oz/2 cups spinach, chopped

PASTRY:
12 sheets filo pastry
oil, for deep-frying

1 To make the filling, heat the oil in a frying pan (skillet) and sauté the onion for 1–2 minutes, stirring until softened. Stir in all of the spices and garlic and cook for 1 minute.

2 Add the potatoes and cook over a gentle heat for 5 minutes, stirring until they begin to soften.

3 Stir in the peas and spinach and cook for a further 3–4 minutes.

4 Lay the filo pastry sheets out on a clean work surface (counter) and fold each sheet in half lengthwise.

5 Place 2 tbsp of the vegetable filling at one end of each folded pastry sheet. Fold over one corner to make a triangle. Continue folding in this way to make a triangular package and seal the edges with water.

6 Repeat with the remaining pastry and filling.

7 Heat the oil for deep-frying to 180°C/350°F or until a cube of bread browns in 30 seconds. Fry the samosas, in batches, for 1–2 minutes until golden. Drain on absorbent paper towels and keep warm whilst cooking the remainder. Serve.

COOK'S TIP

Serve with a yogurt sauce (see page 44) and a salad.

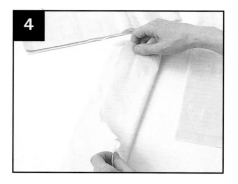

Scrambled Tofu (Bean Curd) on Toast

This is a delicious dish which would also serve as a light lunch or supper.

Serves 4

INGREDIENTS

75 g/2³/₄ oz/6 tbsp vegetarian
   margarine
450 g/1 lb marinated,
   firm tofu (bean curd)

1 red onion, chopped
1 red (bell) pepper, chopped
4 ciabatta rolls
2 tbsp chopped mixed herbs

salt and pepper
fresh herbs, to garnish

1 Melt the margarine in a frying pan (skillet) and crumble the tofu (bean curd) into the pan.

2 Add the onion and (bell) pepper and cook for 3–4 minutes, stirring occasionally.

3 Meanwhile, slice the ciabatta rolls in half and toast under a hot grill (broiler) for about 2–3 minutes, turning once. Remove the toasts and transfer to a serving plate.

4 Add the herbs to the tofu (bean curd) mixture, combine and season.

5 Spoon the tofu (bean curd) mixture on to the toast and garnish with fresh herbs. Serve at once.

COOK'S TIP

Marinated tofu adds extra flavour to this dish. Smoked tofu could be used in its place.

COOK'S TIP

Rub the cut surface of a garlic clove over the toasted ciabatta rolls for extra flavour.

Mixed Bean Pan-Fry

Fresh green beans have a wonderful flavour that is hard to beat.
If you cannot find fresh beans, use thawed, frozen beans instead.

Serves 4

INGREDIENTS

350 g/12 oz/4 cups mixed green
    beans, such as French (green) and
    broad (fava) beans
2 tbsp vegetable oil
2 garlic cloves, crushed
1 red onion, halved and sliced

225 g/8 oz firm marinated
    tofu (bean curd), diced
1 tbsp lemon juice
$^1/_2$ tsp turmeric
1 tsp ground mixed spice

150 ml/$^1/_4$ pint/$^2/_3$ cup vegetable
    stock
2 tsp sesame seeds

1 Trim and chop the French (green) beans and set aside until required.

2 Heat the oil in a frying pan (skillet) and sauté the garlic and onion for 2 minutes, stirring well.

3 Add the tofu (bean curd) and cook for 2–3 minutes until just beginning to brown.

4 Add the French (green) beans and broad (fava) beans. Stir in the lemon juice, turmeric, mixed spice and vegetable stock and bring to the boil.

5 Reduce the heat and simmer for 5–7 minutes or until the beans are tender. Sprinkle with sesame seeds and serve immediately.

VARIATION

Add lime juice instead of lemon, for an alternative citrus flavour.

VARIATION

Use smoked tofu (bean curd) instead of marinated tofu (bean curd) for an alternative flavour.

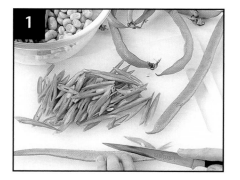

Calzone with Sun-dried Tomatoes & Vegetables

These pizza base parcels are great for making in advance and freezing – they can be defrosted when required for a quick snack.

Makes 4

INGREDIENTS

DOUGH:
450 g/1 lb/3^1/2 cups strong white
    flour
2 tsp easy-blend dried yeast
1 tsp caster (superfine) sugar
150 ml/^{1}/4 pint/^{2}/3 cup vegetable
    stock

150 ml/^{1}/4 pint/^{2}/3 cup passata
    (sieved tomatoes)
beaten egg

FILLING:
1 tbsp vegetable oil
1 onion, chopped
1 garlic clove, crushed
2 tbsp chopped sun-dried tomatoes

100 g/3^1/2 oz spinach, chopped
3 tbsp canned and drained sweetcorn
25 g/1 oz/^{1}/4 cup French (green)
    beans, cut into three
1 tbsp tomato purée (paste)
1 tbsp chopped oregano
50 g/1^3/4 oz Mozzarella cheese, sliced
salt and pepper

1 Sieve the flour into a bowl. Add the yeast and sugar and beat in the stock and passata (sieved tomatoes) to make a smooth dough.

2 Knead the dough on a lightly floured surface for 10 minutes, then place in a clean, lightly oiled bowl and leave to rise in a warm place for 1 hour.

3 Heat the oil in a frying pan (skillet) and sauté the onion for 2–3 minutes. Stir in the garlic, tomatoes, spinach, corn and beans and cook for 3–4 minutes. Add the tomato purée (paste) and oregano and season well.

4 Divide the risen dough into 4 equal portions and roll each on to a floured surface to form an 18 cm/7 inch circle. Spoon a quarter of the filling on to one half of each circle and top with cheese. Fold the dough over to encase the filling, sealing the edge with a fork. Glaze with beaten egg. Put the calzone on a lightly greased baking tray (cookie sheet) and cook in a preheated oven, 220°C/425°F/Gas Mark 7, for 25–30 minutes until risen and golden. Serve warm.

Vegetable Enchiladas

This Mexican dish uses prepared tortillas which are readily available in supermarkets.
They are filled with a spicy vegetable mixture and topped with a hot tomato sauce.

Serves 4

INGREDIENTS

4 flour tortillas
75 g/2^3/$_4$ oz/^{3}/$_4$ cup vegetarian
   Cheddar, grated

FILLING:
75 g/2^3/$_4$ oz spinach
2 tbsp olive oil
8 baby sweetcorn cobs, sliced
25 g/1 oz/1 tbsp frozen peas, thawed

1 red (bell) pepper, diced
1 carrot, diced
1 leek, sliced
2 garlic cloves, crushed
1 red chilli, chopped
salt and pepper

SAUCE:
300 ml/^{1}/$_2$ pint/1^1/$_4$ cups passata
   (sieved tomatoes)
2 shallots, chopped
1 garlic clove, crushed
300 ml/^{1}/$_2$ pint/1^1/$_4$ cups vegetable
   stock
1 tsp caster (superfine) sugar
1 tsp chilli powder

1 To make the filling, blanch the spinach in a pan of boiling water for 2 minutes, drain well and chop.

2 Heat the oil in a frying pan (skillet) and sauté the corn, peas, (bell) pepper, carrot, leek, garlic and chilli for 3–4 minutes, stirring briskly. Stir in the spinach and season well with salt and pepper to taste.

3 Put all of the sauce ingredients in a saucepan and bring to the boil, stirring. Cook over a high heat for 20 minutes, stirring, until thickened and reduced by a third.

4 Spoon a quarter of the filling along the centre of each tortilla. Roll the tortillas around the filling and place in an ovenproof dish, seam-side down.

5 Pour the sauce over the tortillas and sprinkle the cheese on top. Cook in a preheated oven, 180°C/350°F/Gas Mark 4, for 20 minutes or until the cheese has melted and browned. Serve immediately.

Spinach Gnocchi with Tomato & Basil Sauce

These gnocchi or small dumplings are made with potato and flavoured with spinach and nutmeg and served in a rich tomato sauce for an ideal light meal.

Serves 4

INGREDIENTS

450 g/1 lb baking potatoes
75 g/2³/4 oz spinach
1 tsp water
25 g/1 oz/3 tbsp butter or vegetarian
 margarine
1 small egg, beaten

150 g/5¹/2 oz/³/4 cup plain
 (all-purpose) flour
fresh basil sprigs, to garnish

TOMATO SAUCE:
1 tbsp olive oil
1 shallot, chopped

1 tbsp tomato purée (paste)
225 g/8 oz can chopped tomatoes
2 tbsp chopped basil
85 ml/3 fl oz/6 tbsp red wine
1 tsp caster (superfine) sugar
salt and pepper

1 Cook the potatoes in their skins in a pan of boiling salted water for 20 minutes. Drain well and press through a sieve into a bowl. Cook the spinach in 1 tsp water for 5 minutes until wilted. Drain and pat dry with paper towels. Chop and stir into the potatoes.

2 Add the butter or margarine, egg and half of the flour to the potato mixture, mixing well.

Turn out on to a floured surface, gradually kneading in the remaining flour to form a soft dough. With floured hands, roll the dough into thin ropes and cut off 2 cm/³/4 inch pieces. Press the centre of each dumpling with your finger, drawing it towards you to curl the sides of the gnocchi. Cover and leave to chill.

3 Heat the oil for the sauce in a pan and sauté the chopped

shallots for 5 minutes. Add the tomato purée (paste), tomatoes, basil, red wine and sugar and season well. Bring to the boil and then simmer for 20 minutes.

4 Bring a pan of salted water to the boil and cook the gnocchi for 2–3 minutes or until they rise to the top of the pan. Drain well and transfer to serving dishes. Spoon the tomato sauce over the top. Garnish and serve.

Vegetable Jambalaya

*This dish traditionally contains spicy sausage but it is equally delicious
filled with vegetables in this spicy vegetarian version.*

Serves 4

INGREDIENTS

75 g/2³/₄ oz/¹/₂ cup brown rice
2 tbsp olive oil
2 garlic cloves, crushed
1 red onion, cut into eight
1 aubergine (eggplant), diced
1 green (bell) pepper, diced

50 g/1³/₄ oz baby corn cobs,
  halved lengthwise
50 g/1³/₄ oz/¹/₂ cup frozen peas
100 g/3¹/₂ oz small broccoli florets
150 ml/5 floz/²/₃ cup vegetable stock
225 ml/8 fl oz can chopped tomatoes

1 tbsp tomato purée (paste)
1 tsp creole seasoning
¹/₂ tsp chilli flakes
salt and pepper

1 Cook the rice in a saucepan of boiling water for 20 minutes or until cooked through. Drain and set aside.

2 Heat the oil in a heavy-based frying pan (skillet) and cook the garlic and onion for 2–3 minutes, stirring.

3 Add the aubergine (eggplant), (bell) pepper, corn, peas and broccoli to the pan and cook, stirring occasionally, for 2–3 minutes.

4 Stir in the vegetable stock and canned tomatoes, tomato purée (paste), creole seasoning and chilli flakes.

5 Season to taste and cook over a low heat for 15–20 minutes or until the vegetables are tender.

6 Stir the brown rice into the vegetable mixture and cook, mixing well, for 3–4 minutes or until hot. Transfer the vegetable jambalaya to warm serving dishes and serve immediately.

COOK'S TIP

*Use a mixture of rice,
such as wild or red rice, for colour
and texture. Cook the rice in
advance for a speedier recipe.*

Stuffed Mushrooms

Use large open-cap mushrooms for this recipe for their flavour and suitability for filling.

Serves 4

INGREDIENTS

8 open-cap mushrooms
1 tbsp olive oil
1 small leek, chopped
1 celery stick, chopped
100 g/3^1/$_2$ oz firm tofu (bean curd), diced
1 courgette (zucchini), chopped

1 carrot, chopped
100 g/3^1/$_2$ oz/1 cup wholemeal (whole wheat) breadcrumbs
2 tbsp chopped basil
1 tbsp tomato purée (paste)
2 tbsp pine kernels (nuts)

75 g/2^3/$_4$ oz/^{3}/$_4$ cup vegetarian Cheddar cheese, grated
150 ml/^{1}/$_4$ pint/^{2}/$_3$ cup vegetable stock
salt and pepper
green salad, to serve

1 Remove the stalks from the mushrooms and chop finely.

2 Heat the oil in a frying pan (skillet). Add the chopped mushroom stalks, leek, celery, tofu (bean curd), courgette (zucchini) and carrot and cook for 3–4 minutes, stirring.

3 Stir in the breadcrumbs, basil, tomato purée (paste) and pine kernels (nuts). Season with salt and pepper to taste.

4 Spoon the mixture into the mushrooms and top with the cheese.

5 Place the mushrooms in a shallow ovenproof dish and pour the vegetable stock around them.

6 Cook in a preheated oven at 220°C/425°F/Gas Mark 7 for 20 minutes or until cooked through and the cheese has melted. Remove the mushrooms

from the dish and serve immediately with a green salad.

COOK'S TIP

Vary the vegetables used for flavour and colour or according to those you have available.

Vegetable Crêpes

Crêpes or pancakes are ideal for filling with your favourite ingredients. In this recipe they are packed with a spicy vegetable filling which may be made in advance and heated through for serving.

Serves 4

INGREDIENTS

PANCAKES:
100 g/3^1/2 oz plain (all-purpose) flour
pinch of salt
1 egg, beaten
300 ml/^{1}/2 pint/1^1/4 cups milk
vegetable oil, for frying

FILLING:
2 tbsp vegetable oil
1 leek, shredded
^{1}/2 tsp chilli powder
^{1}/2 tsp ground cumin
50 g/1^3/4 oz mangetout (snow peas)
100 g/3^1/2 oz button mushrooms,
1 red (bell) pepper, sliced
25 g/1 oz/^{1}/4 cup cashew nuts,
  chopped

SAUCE:
25 g/1 oz/2 tbsp vegetarian
  margarine
25 g/1 oz/3 tbsp plain
  (all-purpose) flour
150 ml/^{1}/4 pint/^{2}/3 cup vegetable
  stock
150 ml/^{1}/4 pint/^{2}/3 cup milk
1 tsp Dijon mustard
75 g/2^3/4 oz Cheddar cheese, grated
2 tbsp chopped coriander (cilantro)

1 For the pancakes, sieve the flour and salt into a bowl. Beat in the egg and milk to make a batter. For the filling, heat the oil in a pan (skillet) and sauté the leek for 2–3 minutes. Add the rest of the ingredients and cook for 5 minutes, stirring. To make the sauce, melt the margarine in a pan and add the flour. Cook for 1 minute and remove from the heat. Stir in the stock and milk and return to the heat. Bring to the boil, stirring until thick. Add the mustard, half of the cheese and the coriander (cilantro); cook for 1 minute.

2 Heat 1 tbsp of oil in a non-stick 15 cm/6 inch frying pan (skillet). Pour the oil from the pan and add an eighth of the batter, to cover the base of the pan. Cook for 2 minutes, turn the pancake and cook the other side for 1 minute. Repeat with the remaining batter. Spoon a little of the filling along the centre of each pancake and roll up. Place in a heatproof dish and pour the sauce on top. Top with cheese and heat under a hot grill (broiler) for 3–5 minutes or until the cheese melts and turns golden.

Vegetable Pasta Nests

These large pasta nests look impressive when presented filled
with grilled (broiled) mixed vegetables, and taste delicious.

Serves 4

INGREDIENTS

175 g/6 oz spaghetti
1 aubergine (eggplant), halved and
  sliced
1 courgette (zucchini), diced
1 red (bell) pepper, seeded and
  chopped diagonally

6 tbsp olive oil
2 garlic cloves, crushed
50 g/1³/₄ oz/4 tbsp butter or
  vegetarian margarine, melted
15 g/¹/₂ oz/1 tbsp dry white
  breadcrumbs

salt and pepper
fresh parsley sprigs, to garnish

1 Bring a large saucepan of water to the boil and cook the spaghetti until 'al dente' or according to the instructions on the packet. Drain well and set aside until required.

2 Place the aubergine (eggplant), courgette (zucchini) and (bell) pepper on a baking tray (cookie sheet).

3 Mix the oil and garlic together and pour over the vegetables, tossing to coat.

4 Cook under a preheated hot grill (broiler) for about 10 minutes, turning, until tender and lightly charred. Set aside and keep warm.

5 Divide the spaghetti among 4 lightly greased Yorkshire pudding tins (pans). Using a fork, curl the spaghetti to form nests.

6 Brush the pasta nests with melted butter or margarine and sprinkle with the breadcrumbs. Bake in a preheated oven, at 200°C/400°F/ Gas Mark 6, for 15 minutes or until lightly golden. Remove the pasta nests from the tins (pans) and transfer to serving plates. Divide the grilled (broiled) vegetables between the pasta nests, season and garnish.

COOK'S TIP

'Al dente' means 'to the bite' and
describes cooked pasta that is not too
soft, but still has a bite to it.

Vegetable Burgers & Chips

These spicy vegetable burgers are delicious, especially when served with the light oven chips (fries). Serve them in a warm bun or roll with radicchio lettuce leaves and red onion relish.

Serves 4

INGREDIENTS

VEGETABLE BURGERS:
100 g/3^1/2 oz spinach
1 tbsp olive oil
1 leek, chopped
2 garlic cloves, crushed
100 g/3^1/2 oz mushrooms, chopped
300 g/10^1/2 oz firm tofu (bean curd), chopped

1 tsp chilli powder
1 tsp curry powder
1 tbsp chopped coriander (cilantro)
75 g/2^3/4 oz fresh wholemeal (whole wheat) breadcrumbs
1 tbsp olive oil

CHIPS (FRIES):
2 large potatoes
2 tbsp flour
1 tsp chilli powder
2 tbsp olive oil
burger bap or roll and salad, to serve

1 To make the burgers, cook the spinach in a little water for 2 minutes. Drain thoroughly and pat dry with paper towels.

2 Heat the oil in a frying pan (skillet) and sauté the leek and garlic for 2–3 minutes. Add the remaining ingredients except for the breadcrumbs and cook for 5–7 minutes until the vegetables have softened. Toss in the spinach and cook for 1 minute.

3 Transfer the mixture to a food processor and blend for 30 seconds until almost smooth. Stir in the breadcrumbs, mixing well, and leave until cool enough to handle. Using floured hands, form the mixture into four equal-sized burgers. Leave to chill for 30 minutes.

4 To make the chips (fries), cut the potatoes into thin wedges and cook in a pan of boiling water for 10 minutes. Drain and toss in the flour and chilli. Lay the chips on a baking tray (cookie sheet) and sprinkle with the oil. Cook in a preheated oven, 200°C/400°F/Gas Mark 6, for 30 minutes or until golden.

5 Meanwhile, heat 1 tbsp oil in a frying pan (skillet) and cook the burgers for 8–10 minutes, turning once. Serve with salad in a bap.

Vegetable Dim Sum

Dim sum are small Chinese parcels, usually served as part of a large mixed meal.
They may be filled with any variety of fillings, steamed or fried and served with a dipping sauce.

Serves 4

INGREDIENTS

2 spring onions (scallions), chopped
25 g/1 oz green beans, chopped
$^1/_2$ small carrot, finely chopped
1 red chilli, chopped
25 g/1 oz/$^1/_3$ cup bean sprouts, chopped

25 g/1 oz/$^1/_3$ cup button mushrooms, chopped
25 g/1 oz/$^1/_4$ cup unsalted cashew nuts, chopped
1 small egg, beaten
2 tbsp cornflour (cornstarch)

1 tsp light soy sauce
1 tsp hoi-sin sauce
1 tsp sesame oil
32 wonton wrappers
oil, for deep-frying
1 tbsp sesame seeds

1 Mix all of the vegetables together in a bowl.

2 Add the nuts, egg, cornflour (cornstarch), soy sauce, hoi-sin sauce and sesame oil to the bowl, stirring to mix well.

3 Lay the wonton wrappers out on a chopping board and spoon small quantities of the mixture into the centre of each. Gather the wrapper around the filling at the top, to make little parcels, leaving the top open.

4 Heat the oil for deep-frying in a wok to 180°C/350°F or until a cube of bread browns in 30 seconds.

5 Fry the wontons, in batches, for 1–2 minutes or until golden brown. Drain on absorbent paper towels and keep warm whilst frying the remaining wontons.

6 Sprinkle the sesame seeds over the wontons. Serve the vegetable dim sum with a soy or plum dipping sauce.

COOK'S TIP

If preferred, arrange the wontons on a heatproof plate and then steam in a steamer for 5-7 minutes for a healthier cooking method.

Cheese & Garlic Mushroom Pizzas

*This pizza dough is flavoured with garlic and herbs and topped with
mixed mushrooms and melting cheese for a really delicious pizza.*

Serves 4

INGREDIENTS

DOUGH:
450 g/1 lb/3½ cups strong white
   flour
2 tsp easy-blend yeast
2 garlic cloves, crushed
2 tbsp chopped thyme
2 tbsp olive oil

300 ml/½ pint/1¼ cups tepid water

TOPPING:
25 g/1 oz/2 tbsp butter or vegetarian
   margarine
350 g/12 oz mixed mushrooms, sliced
2 garlic cloves, crushed

2 tbsp chopped parsley
2 tbsp tomato purée (paste)
6 tbsp passata (sieved tomatoes)
75 g/2¾ oz Mozzarella cheese,
   grated
salt and pepper
chopped parsley, to garnish

1 Put the flour, yeast, garlic and thyme in a bowl. Make a well in the centre and gradually stir in the oil and water. Bring together to form a soft dough.

2 Turn the dough on to a floured surface and knead for 5 minutes or until smooth. Roll into a 35 cm/14 inch round and place on a greased baking tray (cookie sheet). Leave in a warm place for 20 minutes or until the dough puffs up.

3 Meanwhile, make the topping. Melt the margarine or butter in a frying pan (skillet) and sauté the mushrooms, garlic and parsley for 5 minutes.

4 Mix the tomato purée (paste) and passata (sieved tomatoes) and spoon on to the pizza base, leaving a 1 cm/½ inch edge of dough. Spoon the mushroom mixture on top. Season well and sprinkle the cheese on top. Cook the pizza in a preheated oven,

190°C/375°F/Gas Mark 5, for 20–25 minutes or until the base is crisp and the cheese has melted. Garnish with chopped parsley and serve.

COOK'S TIP

If preferred, spread the base with a prepared cheese sauce before adding the mushrooms.

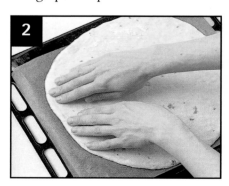

Watercress & Cheese Tartlets

These individual tartlets are great for lunchtime or for picnic food. Watercress is a good source of folic acid, which is important in early pregnancy.

Makes 4

INGREDIENTS

100 g/3$^1\!/_2$ oz/$^3\!/_4$ cup plain (all-purpose) flour
pinch of salt
75 g/2$^3\!/_4$ oz /$^1\!/_2$ cup butter or vegetarian margarine
2–3 tbsp cold water

2 bunches watercress
2 garlic cloves, crushed
1 shallot, chopped
150 g/5$^1\!/_2$ oz vegetarian Cheddar cheese, grated

4 tbsp natural (unsweetened) yogurt
$^1\!/_2$ tsp paprika

1 Sieve the flour into a mixing bowl and add the salt. Rub 50 g/1$^3\!/_4$ oz/$^1\!/_3$ cup of the butter or margarine into the flour until the mixture resembles breadcrumbs.

2 Stir in the cold water to make a dough.

3 Roll the dough out on a floured surface and use to line four 10 cm/4 inch tartlet tins (pans). Prick the bases with a fork and leave to chill.

4 Heat the remaining butter or margarine in a frying pan (skillet). Discard the stems from the watercress and add to the pan with the garlic and shallot, cooking for 1–2 minutes until the watercress is wilted.

5 Remove the pan from the heat and stir in the cheese, yogurt and paprika.

6 Spoon the mixture into the pastry cases and cook in a preheated oven, 180°C/350°F/Gas Mark 4, for 20 minutes or until the filling is firm. Turn out the tartlets and serve.

VARIATION

Use spinach instead of the watercress, making sure it is well drained before mixing with the remaining filling ingredients.

Vegetable-filled Ravioli

*These small parcels are very easy to make and have the advantage of being filled with
your favourite mixture of succulent mushrooms. Serve with freshly grated cheese sprinkled on top.*

Serves 4

INGREDIENTS

FILLING:
25 g/1 oz/3 tbsp butter or
  vegetarian margarine
2 garlic cloves, crushed
1 small leek, chopped
2 celery sticks, chopped

200 g/7 oz/2^1/3 cups open-cap
  mushrooms, chopped
1 egg, beaten
2 tbsp grated vegetarian Parmesan
  cheese
salt and pepper

RAVIOLI:
4 sheets filo pastry
25 g/1 oz/3 tbsp vegetarian
  margarine
oil, for deep-frying

1 To make the filling, melt the butter or margarine in a frying pan (skillet) and sauté the garlic and leek for 2–3 minutes until softened.

2 Add the celery and mushrooms and cook for a further 4–5 minutes until all of the vegetables are tender.

3 Turn off the heat and stir in the egg and grated Parmesan cheese. Season with salt and pepper to taste.

4 Lay the pastry sheets on a chopping board and cut each into nine squares.

5 Spoon a little of the filling into the centre half of the squares and brush the edges of the pastry with butter or margarine. Lay another square on top and seal the edges to make a parcel.

6 Heat the oil for deep-frying to 180°C/350°F or until a cube of bread browns in 30 seconds. Fry the ravioli, in batches, for 2–3 minutes or until golden brown. Remove from the oil with a slotted spoon and pat dry on absorbent paper towels. Transfer to a warm serving plate and serve.

COOK'S TIP

Parmesan cheese is generally non-vegetarian, however, there is an Italian Parmesan called Grano Padano, which is usually vegetarian. Alternatively you could use Pecorino.

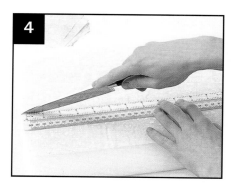

Bulgur-Filled Aubergines (Eggplants)

In this recipe, aubergines (eggplants) are filled with a spicy bulgur wheat and vegetable stuffing for a delicious light meal.

Serves 4

INGREDIENTS

4 medium aubergines (eggplants)
salt
175 g/6 oz/^{3}/$_4$ cup bulgur wheat
300 ml/^{1}/$_2$ pint/1^1/$_4$ cups boiling
   water
3 tbsp olive oil
2 garlic cloves, crushed

2 tbsp pine kernels (nuts)
^{1}/$_2$ tsp turmeric
1 tsp chilli powder
2 celery sticks, chopped
4 spring onions (scallions), chopped
1 carrot, grated

50 g/1^3/$_4$ oz/^{3}/$_4$ cup button
   mushrooms, chopped
2 tbsp raisins
2 tbsp chopped fresh coriander
   (cilantro)
green salad, to serve

1 Cut the aubergines (eggplants) in half lengthwise and scoop out the flesh with a teaspoon. Chop the flesh and set aside. Rub the insides of the aubergines (eggplants) with a little salt and leave to stand for 20 minutes.

2 Meanwhile, put the bulgur wheat in a mixing bowl and pour the boiling water over the top. Leave to stand for 20 minutes or until the water has been absorbed.

3 Heat the oil in a frying pan (skillet). Add the garlic, pine kernels (nuts), turmeric, chilli powder, celery, spring onions (scallions), carrot, mushrooms and raisins and cook for 2–3 minutes.

4 Stir in the reserved aubergine (eggplant) flesh and cook for a further 2–3 minutes. Add the coriander (cilantro), mixing well.

5 Remove the pan from the heat and stir in the bulgur wheat. Rinse the aubergine (eggplant) shells under cold water and pat dry with paper towels.

6 Spoon the bulgur filling into the aubergines (eggplants) and place in a roasting tin (pan). Pour in a little boiling water and cook in a preheated oven, 180°C/350°F/Gas Mark 4, for 15–20 minutes.

7 Serve hot with a green salad.

Lentil Croquettes

These croquettes are ideal served with a crisp salad and a tahini (sesame seed paste) dip.

Serves 4

INGREDIENTS

225 g/8 oz/1¹/₄ cups split red lentils
1 green (bell) pepper, finely chopped
1 red onion, finely chopped
2 garlic cloves, crushed
1 tsp garam masala
¹/₂ tsp chilli powder

1 tsp ground cumin
2 tsp lemon juice
2 tbsp chopped unsalted peanuts
600 ml/1 pint/2¹/₂ cups water
1 egg, beaten
3 tbsp plain (all-purpose) flour

1 tsp turmeric
1 tsp chilli powder
4 tbsp vegetable oil
salt and pepper
salad leaves and fresh herbs, to serve

1 Put the lentils in a large saucepan with the (bell) pepper, onion, garlic, garam masala, chilli powder, ground cumin, lemon juice and peanuts.

2 Add the water and bring to the boil. Reduce the heat and simmer for 30 minutes or until the liquid has been absorbed, stirring occasionally.

3 Remove the mixture from the heat and leave to cool slightly. Beat in the egg and season with salt and pepper to taste. Leave to cool completely.

4 With floured hands, form the mixture into eight oblong shapes.

5 Mix the flour, turmeric and chilli powder together on a small plate. Roll the croquettes in the spiced flour mixture to coat.

6 Heat the oil in a large frying pan (skillet) and cook the croquettes, in batches, for 10 minutes, turning once, until crisp on both sides. Serve the croquettes with salad leaves and fresh herbs.

COOK'S TIP

Other lentils could be used, but they will require soaking and precooking before use. Red lentils are used for speed and convenience.

Refried Beans with Tortillas

Refried beans are a classic Mexican dish and are usually served as an accompaniment. They are, however, delicious when served with warm tortillas and a quick onion relish.

Serves 4

INGREDIENTS

BEANS:
2 tbsp olive oil
1 onion, finely chopped
3 garlic cloves, crushed
1 green chilli, chopped
400 g/14 oz can red kidney
   beans, drained
400 g/14 oz can pinto beans, drained

2 tbsp chopped coriander (cilantro)
150 ml/$^{1}/_{4}$ pint/$^{2}/_{3}$ cup vegetable
   stock
8 wheat tortillas
25 g/1 oz/$^{1}/_{4}$ cup vegetarian Cheddar
   cheese, grated
salt and pepper

RELISH:
4 spring onions (scallions), chopped
1 red onion, chopped
1 green chilli, chopped
1 tbsp garlic wine vinegar
1 tsp caster (superfine) sugar
1 tomato, chopped

1 Heat the oil for the beans in a large frying pan (skillet). Add the onion and sauté for 3–5 minutes. Add the garlic and chilli and cook for 1 minute.

2 Mash the beans with a potato masher and stir into the pan with the coriander (cilantro).

3 Stir in the stock and cook the beans, stirring, for 5 minutes until soft and pulpy.

4 Place the tortillas on a baking tray (cookie sheet) and heat through in a warm oven for 1–2 minutes.

5 Mix the relish ingredients together.

6 Spoon the beans into a serving dish and top with the cheese. Season well. Roll the tortillas and serve with the relish and beans.

COOK'S TIP

Add a little more liquid to the beans when they are cooking if they begin to catch on the bottom of the frying pan (skillet).

Brown Rice, Vegetable & Herb Gratin

This is a really filling dish and therefore does not require an accompaniment. It is very versatile, and could be made with a wide selection of vegetables.

Serves 4

INGREDIENTS

100 g/3½ oz/⅓ cup brown rice
2 tbsp butter or margarine
1 red onion, chopped
2 garlic cloves, crushed
1 carrot, cut into matchsticks

1 courgette (zucchini), sliced
75 g/2¾ oz baby corn cobs, halved lengthwise
2 tbsp sunflower seeds
3 tbsp chopped mixed herbs

100 g/3½ oz/1 cup grated Mozzarella cheese
2 tbsp wholemeal (whole wheat) breadcrumbs
salt and pepper

1 Cook the rice in a saucepan of boiling salted water for 20 minutes. Drain well.

2 Lightly grease a 900 ml/ 1½ pint ovenproof dish.

3 Heat the butter in a frying pan (skillet). Add the onion and cook, stirring, for 2 minutes or until softened.

4 Add the garlic, carrot, courgette (zucchini) and corn cobs and cook for a further 5 minutes, stirring.

5 Mix the rice with the sunflower seeds and mixed herbs and stir into the pan.

6 Stir in half of the Mozzarella cheese and season with salt and pepper to taste.

7 Spoon the mixture into the greased dish and top with the breadcrumbs and remaining cheese. Cook in a preheated oven, 180°C/350°F/Gas Mark 4, for 25–30 minutes or until the cheese begins to turn golden. Serve.

VARIATION

Use an alternative rice, such as basmati, and flavour the dish with curry spices, if you prefer.

Green Lentil &
Mixed Vegetable Pan-fry

The green lentils used in this recipe require soaking but are worth it for the flavour.
If time is short, use red split peas which do not require soaking.

Serves 4

INGREDIENTS

150 g/5^1/2 oz/3^3/4 cups green lentils
4 tbsp butter or vegetarian margarine
2 garlic cloves, crushed
2 tbsp olive oil
1 tbsp cider vinegar
1 red onion, cut into eight

50 g/1^3/4 oz baby corn cobs,
  halved lengthwise
1 yellow (bell) pepper, cut into strips
1 red (bell) pepper, cut into strips
50 g/1^3/4 oz French (green) beans,
  halved

125 ml/4 fl oz/6 tbsp vegetable stock
2 tbsp clear honey
salt and pepper
crusty bread, to serve

1 Soak the lentils in a large saucepan of cold water for 25 minutes. Bring to the boil, reduce the heat and simmer for 20 minutes. Drain thoroughly.

2 Add 1 tablespoon of the butter or margarine, 1 garlic clove, 1 tablespoon of oil and the vinegar to the lentils and mix well.

3 Melt the remaining butter, garlic and oil in a frying pan (skillet) and stir-fry the onion, corn cobs, (bell) peppers and beans for 3–4 minutes.

4 Add the vegetable stock and bring to the boil for about 10 minutes or until the liquid has evaporated.

5 Add the honey and season with salt and pepper to taste. Stir in the lentil mixture and cook for 1 minute to heat through.

Spoon on to warmed serving plates and serve with crusty bread.

VARIATION

This pan-fry is very versatile – you can use a mixture of your favourite vegetables, if you prefer. Try courgettes (zucchini), carrots or mangetout (snow peas).

Falafel

These are a very tasty, well-known Middle Eastern dish of small chick-pea (garbanzo bean) based balls, spiced and deep-fried. They are delicious hot with a crisp tomato salad.

Serves 4

INGREDIENTS

650 g/1 lb 7 oz/6 cups canned chick-peas (garbanzo beans), drained
1 red onion, chopped
3 garlic cloves, crushed
100 g/3^1/$_2$ oz wholemeal (whole wheat) bread

2 small red chillies
1 tsp ground cumin
1 tsp ground coriander
^{1}/$_2$ tsp turmeric
1 tbsp chopped coriander (cilantro), plus extra to garnish

1 egg, beaten
100 g/3^1/$_2$ oz/1 cup wholemeal (whole wheat) breadcrumbs
vegetable oil, for deep-frying
salt and pepper
tomato and cucumber salad and lemon wedges, to serve

1 Put the chick-peas (garbanzo beans), onion, garlic, bread, chillies, spices and coriander (cilantro) in a food processor and blend for 30 seconds. Stir and season well.

2 Remove the mixture from the food processor and shape into walnut-sized balls.

3 Place the beaten egg in a shallow bowl and place the wholemeal (wholewheat) breadcrumbs on a plate. Dip the balls into the egg to coat and then roll them in the breadcrumbs, shaking off any excess.

4 Heat the oil for deep-frying to 180°C/350°F or until a cube of bread browns in 30 seconds. Fry the falafel, in batches, for 2–3 minutes until crisp and browned. Remove from the oil with a slotted spoon and dry on absorbent paper towels. Garnish with coriander (cilantro) and serve with a tomato and cucumber salad and lemon wedges.

COOK'S TIP

Serve the falafel with a coriander (cilantro) and yogurt sauce. Mix 150 ml/^{1}/$_4$ pint/^{2}/$_3$ cup natural (unsweetened) yogurt with 2 tbsp chopped coriander (cilantro) and 1 crushed garlic clove.

Cabbage & Walnut Stir-Fry

*This is a really quick, one-pan dish using white
and red cabbage for colour and flavour.*

Serves 4

INGREDIENTS

350 g/12 oz white cabbage
350 g/12 oz red cabbage
4 tbsp peanut oil
1 tbsp walnut oil
2 garlic cloves, crushed
8 spring onions (scallions), trimmed

225 g/8 oz firm tofu (bean curd),
   cubed
2 tbsp lemon juice
100 g/3^1/$_2$ oz walnut halves
2 tsp Dijon mustard
2 tsp poppy seeds

salt and pepper

1 Using a sharp knife, shred the white and red cabbages thinly and set aside until required.

2 Heat the peanut and walnut oils in a preheated wok. Add the garlic, cabbage, spring onions (scallions) and tofu (bean curd) and cook for 5 minutes, stirring.

3 Add the lemon juice, walnuts and mustard, season with salt and pepper and cook for a further 5 minutes or until the cabbage is tender.

4 Transfer the stir-fry to a warm serving bowl, sprinkle with poppy seeds and serve.

COOK'S TIP

As well as adding protein, vitamins and useful fats to the diet, nuts and seeds add flavour and texture to vegetarian meals. Keep a good supply of them in your store-cupboard as they can be used in a great variety of dishes – salads, bakes, stir-fries to name but a few.

VARIATION

Sesame seeds could be used instead of the poppy seeds and drizzle 1 teaspoon of sesame oil over the dish just before serving, if you wish.

Spinach Frittata

A frittata is another word for a large, thick omelette. This is an Italian dish which may be made with many flavourings. Spinach is used as the main ingredient in this recipe for colour and flavour.

Serves 4

INGREDIENTS

450 g/1 lb spinach
2 tsp water
4 eggs, beaten
2 tbsp single (light) cream
2 garlic cloves, crushed

50 g/1^3/$_4$ oz/^{3}/$_4$ cup canned
    sweetcorn, drained
1 celery stick, chopped
1 red chilli, chopped
2 tomatoes, seeded and diced
2 tbsp olive oil

2 tbsp butter
25 g/1 oz/^{1}/$_4$ cup pecan nut halves
2 tbsp grated Pecorino cheese
25 g/1 oz/^{1}/$_4$ cup Fontina cheese,
    cubed
a pinch of paprika

1 Cook the spinach in 2 teaspoons of water in a covered pan for 5 minutes. Drain thoroughly and pat dry on absorbent paper towels.

2 Beat the eggs in a bowl and stir in the spinach, single (light) cream, garlic, sweetcorn, celery, chilli and tomatoes until the ingredients are well mixed.

3 Heat the oil and butter in a 20 cm/8 inch heavy-based frying pan (skillet).

4 Spoon the egg mixture into the frying pan (skillet) and sprinkle with the pecan nut halves, Pecorino and Fontina cheeses and paprika. Cook without stirring over a medium heat for 5–7 minutes or until the underside of the frittata is brown.

5 Put a large plate over the pan and invert to turn out the frittata. Slide it back into the frying pan (skillet) and cook the other side for a further 2–3 minutes. Serve the frittata straight from the frying pan (skillet) or transfer to a serving plate.

COOK'S TIP

Be careful not to burn the underside of the frittata during the initial cooking stage – this is why it is important to use a heavy-based frying pan (skillet). Add a little extra oil to the pan when you turn the frittata over if required.

Marinated Grilled (Broiled) Fennel

Fennel has a wonderful aniseed flavour which is ideal for grilling (broiling) or barbecuing (grilling). Marinated in lime, garlic, oil and mustard, this recipe is really delicious.

Serves 4

INGREDIENTS

2 fennel bulbs
1 red (bell) pepper, cut into large
   cubes
1 lime, cut into eight wedges

MARINADE:
2 tbsp lime juice
4 tbsp olive oil
2 garlic cloves, crushed
1 tsp wholegrain mustard
1 tbsp chopped thyme

fennel fronds, to garnish
crisp salad, to serve

1 Cut each of the fennel bulbs into eight pieces and place in a shallow dish. Mix in the (bell) peppers.

2 To make the marinade, combine the lime juice, oil, garlic, mustard and thyme. Pour the marinade over the fennel and (bell) peppers and leave to marinate for 1 hour.

3 Thread the fennel and (bell) peppers on to wooden skewers with the lime wedges.

Preheat a grill (broiler) to medium and grill (broil) the kebabs (kabobs) for 10 minutes, turning and basting with the marinade.

4 Transfer to serving plates, garnish with fennel fronds and serve with a crisp salad.

VARIATION

Substitute 2 tbsp orange juice for the lime juice and add 1 tbsp honey, if you prefer.

COOK'S TIP

Soak the skewers in water for 20 minutes before using to prevent them from burning during cooking.

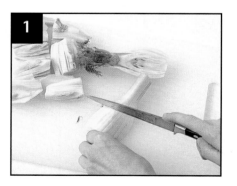

Ciabatta Rolls

Sandwiches are always a welcome snack but can be quite mundane. These crisp ciabatta rolls filled with roast (bell) peppers and cheese are irresistible and will always be a popular light meal.

Serves 4

INGREDIENTS

4 ciabatta rolls
2 tbsp olive oil
1 garlic clove crushed

FILLING:
1 red (bell) pepper
1 green (bell) pepper
1 yellow (bell) pepper
4 radishes, sliced
1 bunch watercress
100 g/3^{1}/$_{2}$ oz/8 tbsp cream cheese

1 Slice the ciabatta rolls in half. Heat the olive oil and crushed garlic in a saucepan. Pour the garlic and oil mixture over the cut surfaces of the rolls and leave to stand.

2 Halve the (bell) peppers and place, skin side uppermost, on a grill (broiler) rack. Cook under a hot grill (broiler) for 8–10 minutes until just beginning to char. Remove the (bell) peppers from the grill (broiler), peel and slice thinly.

3 Arrange the radish slices on one half of each roll with a few watercress leaves. Spoon the cream cheese on top. Pile the (bell) peppers on top of the cream cheese and top with the other half of the roll. Serve.

COOK'S TIP

To peel (bell) peppers, wrap them in foil after grilling (broiling). This traps the steam, loosening the skins and making them easier to peel.

COOK'S TIP

Allow the (bell) peppers to cool slightly before filling the roll otherwise the cheese will melt.

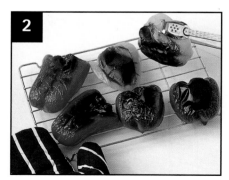

Main Meals

This is the most comprehensive chapter in the book, being perhaps the most important. In a vegetarian diet it is essential to eat a good balance of foods and the following recipes make good use of pulses (legumes), grains, tofu (bean curd) and vegetables to aid in this quest. The recipes in this chapter will enable you to build a balanced, nutritious and flavourful menu which will meet all of your needs.

Anyone who ever thought that vegetarian meals were dull will be proved wrong by the rich variety of dishes in this chapter. You'll recognize influences from Indian, Mexican and Chinese cooking, but there are also traditional stews and casseroles as well as hearty bakes and roasts. They all make exciting eating at any time of year, at virtually any occasion. There are ideas for mid-week meals or for entertaining, some traditional and some more unusual. Don't be afraid to substitute ingredients where appropriate. There is no reason why you cannot enjoy experimenting and adding your own touch to these imaginative ideas.

Mushroom & Spinach Puff Pastry

*These puff parcels are easy to make and delicious to eat. Filled with garlic,
mushrooms and spinach they are ideal with a fresh tomato or cheese sauce.*

Serves 4

INGREDIENTS

2 tbsp butter
1 red onion, halved and sliced
2 garlic cloves, crushed
225 g/8 oz/3 cups open-cap
   mushrooms, sliced

175 g/6 oz baby spinach
pinch of nutmeg
4 tbsp double (heavy) cream
225 g/8 oz prepared puff pastry
1 egg, beaten

salt and pepper
2 tsp poppy seeds

1 Melt the butter in a frying
pan (skillet). Add the onion
and garlic to the pan and sauté for
3–4 minutes, stirring well, until
the onion has softened.

2 Add the mushrooms, spinach
and nutmeg and cook for a
further 2–3 minutes.

3 Stir in the double (heavy)
cream, mixing well.

4 Season with salt and pepper
to taste and remove the pan
from the heat.

5 Roll the pastry out on a lightly
floured surface and cut into
four 15 cm/6 inch circles.

6 Spoon a quarter of the filling
on to one half of each circle
and fold the pastry over to encase
the filling. Press down to seal the
edges of the pastry and brush with
the beaten egg. Sprinkle with the
poppy seeds.

7 Place the parcels on to a
dampened baking tray (cookie
sheet) and cook in a preheated
oven, 200°C/400°F/Gas Mark 6,

for 20 minutes until risen and
golden brown.

8 Transfer the mushroom and
spinach puff pastry parcels to
serving plates and serve
immediately.

COOK'S TIP

*The baking tray (cookie sheet) is
dampened so that steam forms with
the heat of the oven and helps the
pastry to rise and set.*

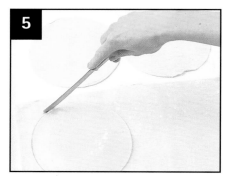

Chick-pea (Garbanzo Bean) Roast with Sherry Sauce

This is a vegetarian version of the classic 'Beef Wellington', and just as delicious.
Served with a sherry sauce and roast vegetables it makes a tasty and impressive main dish.

Serves 4

INGREDIENTS

450 g/1 lb can chick-peas (garbanzo beans), drained
1 tsp marmite (yeast extract)
150 g/5^{1}/2 oz/1^{1}/4 cups chopped walnuts
150 g/5^{1}/2 oz/1^{1}/4 cups fresh white breadcrumbs
1 onion, finely chopped
100 g/3^{1}/2 oz/1^{1}/4 cups mushrooms, sliced

50 g/1^{3}/4 oz canned sweetcorn, drained
2 garlic cloves, crushed
2 tbsp dry sherry
2 tbsp vegetable stock
1 tbsp chopped coriander (cilantro)
225 g/8 oz prepared puff pastry
1 egg, beaten
2 tbsp milk
salt and pepper

SAUCE:
1 tbsp vegetable oil
1 leek, thinly sliced
4 tbsp dry sherry
150 ml/^{1}/4 pint/^{2}/3 cup vegetable stock

1 Blend the chick-peas (garbanzo beans), marmite, nuts and breadcrumbs in a food processor for 30 seconds. In a frying pan (skillet) sauté the onion and mushrooms in their own juices for 3–4 minutes. Stir in the chick-pea mixture, corn and garlic. Add the sherry, stock, coriander and seasoning and bind the mixture together. Remove from the heat and allow to cool.

2 Roll the pastry out on to a lightly floured surface to form a 35.5 cm/14 inch × 30 cm/12 inch rectangle. Shape the chick-pea mixture into a loaf shape and wrap the pastry around it, sealing the edges. Place seam-side down on a dampened baking tray and score the top in a criss-cross pattern. Mix the egg and milk and brush over the pastry. Cook in a preheated oven, 200°C/ 400°F/Gas Mark 6, for 25–30 minutes. Heat the oil for the sauce in a pan and sauté the leek for 5 minutes. Add the sherry and stock, bring to the boil. Simmer for 5 minutes and serve with the roast.

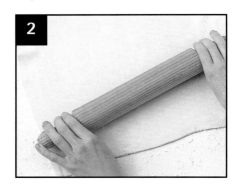
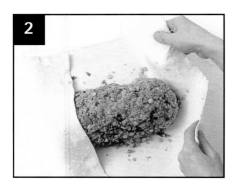

Kidney Bean Kiev

This is a vegetarian version of chicken kiev, the bean patties taking the place of the chicken.
Topped with garlic and herb butter and coated in breadcrumbs, this version is just as delicious.

Serves 4

INGREDIENTS

GARLIC BUTTER:
100 g/3^1/2 oz/ 8 tbsp butter
3 garlic cloves, crushed
1 tbsp chopped parsley

BEAN PATTIES:
650 g/1 lb 7 oz canned red kidney
  beans
150 g/5^1/2 oz/1^1/4 cups fresh white
  breadcrumbs
25 g/1 oz/2 tbsp butter

1 leek, chopped
1 celery stick, chopped
1 tbsp chopped parsley
1 egg, beaten
salt and pepper
vegetable oil, for shallow frying

1 To make the garlic butter, put the butter, garlic and parsley in a bowl and blend together with a wooden spoon. Place the garlic butter mixture on to a sheet of baking parchment, roll into a cigar shape and wrap in the baking parchment. Leave to chill in the refrigerator.

2 Using a potato masher, mash the red kidney beans in a mixing bowl and stir in 75 g/ 2^3/4 oz/^{3}/4 cup of the breadcrumbs until thoroughly blended.

3 Melt the butter in a frying pan (skillet) and sauté the leek and celery for 3–4 minutes, stirring.

4 Add the bean mixture to the pan together with the parsley, season with salt and pepper to taste and mix well. Remove from the heat and leave to cool slightly.

5 Shape the bean mixture into 4 equal sized ovals.

6 Slice the garlic butter into 4 and place a slice in the centre of each bean patty. Mould the bean mixture around the garlic butter to encase it completely.

7 Dip each bean patty into the beaten egg to coat and then roll in the remaining breadcrumbs.

8 Heat a little oil in a frying pan (skillet) and fry the patties, turning once, for 7–10 minutes or until golden. Serve.

Cashew Nut Paella

Paella traditionally contains chicken and fish, but this recipe is packed with vegetables and nuts for a truly delicious and simple vegetarian dish.

Serves 4

INGREDIENTS

2 tbsp olive oil
1 tbsp butter
1 red onion, chopped
150 g/5^1/$_2$ oz/1 cup arborio rice
1 tsp ground turmeric
1 tsp ground cumin
^{1}/$_2$ tsp chilli powder
3 garlic cloves, crushed
1 green chilli, sliced

1 green (bell) pepper, diced
1 red (bell) pepper, diced
75 g/2^3/$_4$ oz baby corn cobs, halved lengthwise
2 tbsp pitted black olives
1 large tomato, seeded and diced
450 ml/^{3}/$_4$ pint/2 cups vegetable stock

75 g/2^3/$_4$ oz/^{3}/$_4$ cup unsalted cashew nuts
25 g/1 oz/^{1}/$_4$ cup frozen peas
2 tbsp chopped parsley
pinch of cayenne pepper
salt and pepper
fresh herbs, to garnish

1 Heat the olive oil and butter in a large frying pan (skillet) or paella pan until the butter has melted.

2 Add the chopped onion to the pan and sauté for 2–3 minutes, stirring, until the onion has softened.

3 Stir in the rice, turmeric, cumin, chilli powder, garlic, chilli, (bell) peppers, corn cobs, olives and tomato and cook over a medium heat for 1–2 minutes, stirring occasionally.

4 Pour in the stock and bring the mixture to the boil. Reduce the heat and cook for 20 minutes, stirring.

5 Add the cashew nuts and peas to the mixture in the pan and cook for a further 5 minutes, stirring occasionally. Season to taste and sprinkle with parsley and cayenne pepper. Transfer to warm serving plates, garnish and serve immediately.

COOK'S TIP

For authenticity and flavour, use a few saffron strands soaked in a little boiling water instead of the turmeric. Saffron has a lovely, nutty flavour.

Vegetable & Tofu Strudels

These strudels look really impressive and are perfect if friends are coming round or for a more formal dinner party dish.

Serves 4

INGREDIENTS

FILLING:
2 tbsp vegetable oil
2 tbsp butter or vegetarian margarine
150 g/5^1/$_2$ oz/^{1}/$_3$ cup potatoes finely diced
1 leek, shredded
2 garlic cloves, crushed

1 tsp garam masala
^{1}/$_2$ tsp chilli powder
^{1}/$_2$ tsp turmeric
50 g/1^3/$_4$ oz okra, sliced
100 g/3^1/$_2$ oz/1^1/$_4$ cups button mushrooms, sliced

2 tomatoes, diced
225 g/8 oz firm tofu (bean curd), diced
12 sheets filo pastry
2 tbsp butter or vegetarian margarine, melted
salt and pepper

---

1 To make the filling, heat the oil and butter in a frying pan (skillet). Add the potatoes and leek and cook for 2–3 minutes, stirring.

2 Add the garlic and spices, okra, mushrooms, tomatoes, tofu (bean curd) and seasoning and cook, stirring, for 5–7 minutes or until tender.

3 Lay the pastry out on a chopping board and brush each individual sheet with butter.

Place 3 sheets on top of one another; repeat to make 4 stacks.

4 Spoon a quarter of the filling along the centre of each stack and brush the edges with butter. Fold the short edges in and roll up lengthwise to form a cigar shape; brush the outside with butter. Place the strudels on a greased baking tray (cookie sheet).

5 Cook in a preheated oven, 190°C/375°F/Gas Mark 5, and cook the strudels for 20 minutes or until golden brown. Serve immediately.

COOK'S TIP

Decorate the outside of the strudels with crumpled pastry trimmings before cooking for a really impressive effect.

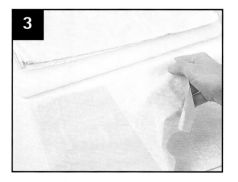

Vegetable Lasagne

This colourful and tasty lasagne, with layers of vegetables in tomato sauce and aubergines (eggplants), all topped with a rich cheese sauce is simply delicious.

Serves 4

INGREDIENTS

1 aubergine (eggplant), sliced	$1/2$ tsp chilli powder	CHEESE SAUCE:
3 tbsp olive oil	$1/2$ tsp ground cumin	2 tbsp butter or vegetarian margarine
2 garlic cloves, crushed	2 tomatoes, chopped	1 tbsp flour
1 red onion, halved and sliced	300 ml/$1/2$ pint/$1^1/4$ cups passata	150 ml/$1/4$ pint/$2/3$ cup vegetable
1 green (bell) pepper, diced	(sieved tomatoes)	stock
1 red (bell) pepper, diced	2 tbsp chopped basil	300 ml/$1/2$ pint/$1^1/4$ cups milk
1 yellow (bell) pepper, diced	8 no pre-cook lasagne verdi sheets	75 g/$2^3/4$ oz/$3/4$ cup vegetarian
225 g/8 oz mixed mushrooms, sliced	salt and pepper	Cheddar, grated
2 celery sticks, sliced		1 tsp Dijon mustard
1 courgette (zucchini), diced		1 tbsp chopped basil
		1 egg, beaten

1 Place the aubergine (eggplant) slices in a colander, sprinkle with salt and leave for 20 minutes. Rinse under cold water, drain and reserve. Heat the oil in a pan and sauté the garlic and onion for 1–2 minutes. Add the (bell) peppers, mushrooms, celery and courgette (zucchini) and cook for 3–4 minutes, stirring. Stir in the spices and cook for 1 minute. Mix the tomatoes, passata (sieved tomatoes) and basil together and season well.

2 For the sauce, melt the butter in a pan, add the flour and cook for 1 minute. Remove from the heat and stir in the stock and milk. Return to the heat and add half of the cheese and the mustard. Boil, stirring, until thickened. Stir in the basil and season. Remove from the heat and stir in the egg. Place half of the lasagne sheets in an ovenproof dish. Top with half of the vegetables, then half of the tomato sauce. Cover with half the aubergines (eggplants). Repeat and spoon the cheese sauce on top. Sprinkle with cheese and cook in a preheated oven, 180°C/350°F/ Gas 4, for 40 minutes.

Lentil & Rice Casserole

*This is a really hearty dish, perfect for cold days
when a filling hot dish is just what you need.*

Serves 4

INGREDIENTS

225 g/8 oz/1^1/4 cups red split lentils
50 g/1^3/4 oz/^{1}/3 cup long-grain white
 rice
1 litre/1^3/4 pints/5 cups vegetable
 stock
150 ml/^{1}/4 pint/^{2}/3 cup dry white
 wine
1 leek, cut into chunks
3 garlic cloves, crushed

400 g/14 oz can chopped tomatoes
1 tsp ground cumin
1 tsp chilli powder
1 tsp garam masala
1 red (bell) pepper, sliced
100 g/3^1/2 oz small broccoli florets
8 baby corn cobs, halved lengthwise
50 g/1^3/4 oz French (green) beans,
 halved

1 tbsp fresh basil, shredded
salt and pepper
fresh basil sprigs, to garnish

1 Place the lentils, rice, vegetable stock and white wine in a flameproof casserole dish and cook over a gentle heat for 20 minutes, stirring occasionally.

2 Add the leek, garlic, tomatoes, cumin, chilli powder, garam masala, (bell) pepper, broccoli, corn cobs and French (green) beans.

3 Bring the mixture to the boil, reduce the heat, cover and simmer for a further 10–15 minutes or until the vegetables are tender.

4 Add the shredded basil and season with salt and pepper to taste.

5 Garnish with fresh basil sprigs and serve immediately.

VARIATION

You can vary the rice in this recipe – use brown or wild rice, if you prefer.

Vegetable Hot Pot

*In this recipe, a variety of vegetables are cooked under a layer of potatoes,
topped with cheese and cooked until golden brown for a filling and tasty meal.*

Serves 4

INGREDIENTS

2 large potatoes, thinly sliced
2 tbsp vegetable oil
1 red onion, halved and sliced
1 leek, sliced
2 garlic cloves, crushed
1 carrot, cut into chunks
100 g/3^1/$_2$ oz broccoli florets

100 g/3^1/$_2$ oz cauliflower florets
2 small turnips, quartered
1 tbsp plain (all-purpose) flour
700 ml/1^1/$_4$ pints/3^1/$_2$ cups vegetable
   stock
150 ml/^{1}/$_4$ pint/^{2}/$_3$ cup dry cider
1 dessert (eating) apple, sliced

2 tbsp chopped sage
pinch of cayenne pepper
50 g/1^3/$_4$ oz/^{1}/$_2$ cup vegetarian
   Cheddar cheese, grated
salt and pepper

1 Cook the potato slices in a
saucepan of boiling water for
10 minutes. Drain thoroughly
and reserve.

2 Heat the oil in a flameproof
casserole dish and sauté the
onion, leek and garlic for
2–3 minutes. Add the remaining
vegetables and cook for a further
3–4 minutes, stirring.

3 Stir in the flour and cook for
1 minute. Gradually add the
stock and cider and bring the
mixture to the boil. Add the apple,
sage and cayenne pepper and
season well. Remove the dish from
the heat. Transfer the vegetables to
an ovenproof dish.

4 Arrange the potato slices on
top of the vegetable mixture
to cover.

5 Sprinkle the cheese on top of
the potato slices and cook in a
preheated oven, 190°C/375°F/Gas
Mark 5, for 30–35 minutes or
until the potato is golden brown
and beginning to crispen
slightly around the edges.
Serve immediately.

COOK'S TIP

*If the potato begins to
brown too quickly, cover with
foil for the last 10 minutes of
cooking time to prevent the
top from burning.*

Vegetable Chop Suey

A classic Chinese dish found on all take-away menus,
this recipe is quick to prepare and makes a tasty meal.

Serves 4

INGREDIENTS

2 tbsp peanut oil
1 onion, chopped
3 garlic cloves, chopped
1 green (bell) pepper, diced
1 red (bell) pepper, diced
75 g/2³/₄ oz broccoli florets

1 courgette (zucchini), sliced
25 g/1 oz French (green) beans
1 carrot, cut into matchsticks
100 g/3¹/₂ oz bean sprouts
2 tsp light brown sugar
2 tbsp light soy sauce

125 ml/4 fl oz/¹/₂ cup vegetable stock
salt and pepper
noodles, to serve

1 Heat the oil in a preheated wok until almost smoking. Add the onion and garlic and stir-fry for 30 seconds.

2 Stir in the (bell) peppers, broccoli, courgette (zucchini), beans and carrot and stir-fry for a further 2–3 minutes.

3 Add the bean sprouts, light brown sugar, soy sauce and vegetable stock. Season with salt and pepper to taste and cook for about 2 minutes.

4 Transfer the vegetables to serving plates and serve immediately with noodles.

COOK'S TIP

The clever design of a wok, with its spherical base and high sloping sides, enables the food to be tossed so that it is cooked quickly and evenly. It is essential to heat the wok sufficiently before you add the ingredients to ensure quick and even cooking.

COOK'S TIP

Ensure that the vegetable pieces are of the same size in order that they all cook in the stated time.

VARIATION

Add 1 tbsp chilli oil for a hotter flavour and add cashew nuts for extra crunch.

Vegetable Toad-in-the-hole

This dish can be made in one large dish or in individual Yorkshire pudding tins (pans).

Serves 4

INGREDIENTS

BATTER:
100 g/3^{1}/$_{2}$ oz/^{3}/$_{4}$ cup plain (all-purpose) flour
2 eggs, beaten
200 ml/7 fl oz/^{3}/$_{4}$ cup milk
2 tbsp wholegrain mustard
2 tbsp vegetable oil

FILLING:
2 tbsp butter
2 garlic cloves, crushed
1 onion, cut into eight
75 g/2^{3}/$_{4}$ oz baby carrots, halved lengthwise
50 g/1^{3}/$_{4}$ oz French (green) beans

50 g/1^{3}/$_{4}$ oz canned sweetcorn, drained
2 tomatoes, seeded and cut into chunks
1 tsp wholegrain mustard
1 tbsp chopped mixed herbs
salt and pepper

1 To make the batter, sieve the flour and a pinch of salt into a large bowl. Make a well in the centre and beat in the eggs and milk to make a batter. Stir in the mustard and leave to stand.

2 Pour the oil into a shallow ovenproof dish and heat in a preheated oven, 200°C/400°F/Gas Mark 6, for 10 minutes.

3 To make the filling, melt the butter in a frying pan (skillet) and sauté the garlic and onion for 2 minutes, stirring. Cook the carrots and beans in a saucepan of boiling water for 7 minutes or until tender. Drain well.

4 Add the sweetcorn and tomato to the frying pan (skillet) with the mustard and herbs. Season well and add the carrots and beans.

5 Remove the dish from the oven and pour in the batter. Spoon the vegetables into the centre, return to the oven and cook for 30–35 minutes until the batter has risen and set. Serve the vegetable toad-in-the-hole immediately.

COOK'S TIP

It is important that the oil is hot before adding the batter so that the batter begins to cook and rise immediately.

Vegetable Jalousie

This is a really easy dish to make, but looks impressive.
The mixture of vegetables gives the dish a wonderful colour and flavour.

Serves 4

INGREDIENTS

450 g/1 lb prepared puff pastry
1 egg, beaten

FILLING:
2 tbsp butter or vegetarian margarine
1 leek, shredded

2 garlic cloves, crushed
1 red (bell) pepper, sliced
1 yellow (bell) pepper, sliced
50 g/1³/4 oz mushrooms, sliced
75 g/2³/4 oz small asparagus spears
2 tbsp flour

85 ml/3 fl oz/6 tbsp vegetable stock
85 ml/3 fl oz/6 tbsp milk
4 tbsp dry white wine
1 tbsp chopped oregano
salt and pepper

1 Melt the butter or margarine in a pan and sauté the leek and garlic for 2 minutes, stirring. Add the remaining vegetables and cook, stirring, for 3–4 minutes.

2 Add the flour and cook for 1 minute. Remove the pan from the heat and stir in the vegetable stock, milk and white wine. Return the pan to the heat and bring to the boil, stirring, until thickened. Stir in the oregano and season with salt and pepper to taste.

3 Roll half of the pastry out on a lightly floured surface to form a rectangle 42.5 cm/15 inches × 15 cm/6 inches.

4 Roll out the other half of the pastry to the same shape, but a little larger. Put the smaller rectangle on a baking tray (cookie sheet) lined with dampened baking parchment.

5 Spoon the filling on top of the smaller rectangle, leaving a 1.25 cm/½ inch clean edge.

6 Cut parallel slits across the larger rectangle to within 2.5 cm/1 inch of each edge.

7 Brush the edge of the smaller rectangle with egg and place the larger rectangle on top, sealing the edges well.

8 Brush the whole jalousie with egg and cook in a preheated oven, 200°C/400°F/Gas Mark 6, for 30–35 minutes until risen and golden. Serve immediately.

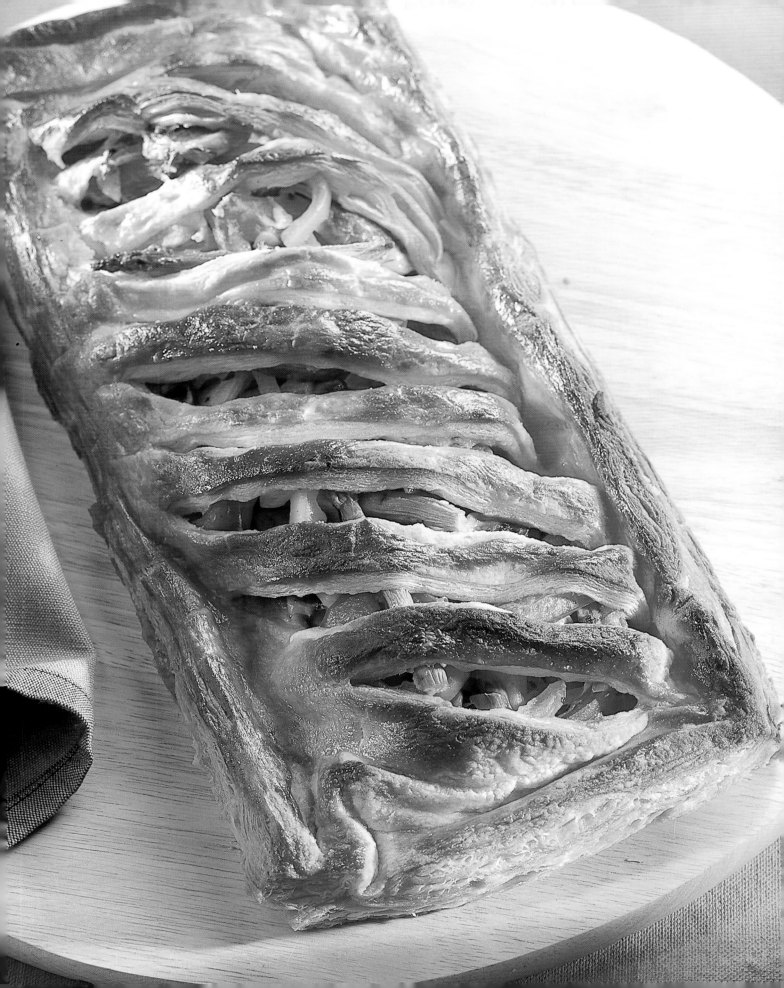

Cauliflower, Broccoli & Cheese Flan

This really is a tasty flan, the pastry case for which may be made in advance and frozen until required.

Serves 8

INGREDIENTS

PASTRY:
175 g/6 oz/1¼ cups plain (all-purpose) flour
pinch of salt
½ tsp paprika
1 tsp dried thyme
75 g/2¾ oz/6 tbsp vegetarian margarine

3 tbsp water

FILLING:
100 g/3½ oz cauliflower florets
100 g/3½ oz broccoli florets
1 onion, cut into eight
2 tbsp butter or vegetarian margarine
1 tbsp plain (all-purpose) flour

85 ml/3 fl oz/6 tbsp vegetable stock
125 ml/4 fl oz/8 tbsp milk
75 g/2¾ oz/¾ cup vegetarian Cheddar cheese, grated
salt and pepper
paprika and thyme, to garnish

1 To make the pastry, sieve the flour and salt into a bowl. Add the paprika and thyme and rub in the margarine. Stir in the water and bind to form a dough.

2 Roll the pastry out on a floured surface and use to line an 18cm/7 inch loose-bottomed flan tin (pan). Prick the base with a fork and line with baking parchment. Fill with ceramic baking beans and bake in a preheated oven, at 190°C/375°F/Gas Mark 5, for 15 minutes. Remove the parchment and beans and return the pastry case to the oven for 5 minutes.

3 To make the filling, cook the vegetables in a pan of boiling water for 10–12 minutes until tender. Drain and reserve.

4 Melt the butter in a pan. Add the flour and cook, stirring, for 1 minute. Remove from the heat, stir in the stock and milk and return to the heat. Bring to the boil, stirring, and add 50 g/1¾ oz/½ cup of the cheese. Season.

5 Spoon the cauliflower, broccoli and onion into the pastry case. Pour over the sauce and sprinkle with the cheese. Return to the oven for 10 minutes until the cheese is bubbling. Dust with paprika, garnish and serve.

Roast (Bell) Pepper Tart

This tastes truly delicious, the flavour of roasted vegetables being entirely different from that of boiled or fried.

Serves 8

INGREDIENTS

PASTRY:
175 g/6 oz/1^{1}/$_{4}$ cups plain (all-purpose) flour
pinch of salt
75 g/2^{3}/$_{4}$ oz/6 tbsp butter or vegetarian margarine
2 tbsp green pitted olives, finely chopped

3 tbsp cold water

FILLING:
1 red (bell) pepper
1 green (bell) pepper
1 yellow (bell) pepper
2 garlic cloves, crushed
2 tbsp olive oil

100 g/3^{1}/$_{2}$ oz/1 cup Mozzarella cheese, grated
2 eggs
150 ml/5 fl oz/^{2}/$_{3}$ cup milk
1 tbsp chopped basil
salt and pepper

1 To make the pastry, sieve the flour and a pinch of salt into a bowl. Rub in the butter or margarine until the mixture resembles breadcrumbs. Add the olives and cold water, bringing the mixture together to form a dough.

2 Roll the dough out on to a floured surface and use to line a 20 cm/8 inch loose-bottomed flan tin (pan). Prick the base with a fork and leave to chill.

3 Cut the (bell) peppers in half lengthwise and lay skin-side uppermost on a baking tray (cookie sheet). Mix the garlic and oil and brush over the (bell) peppers. Cook in a preheated oven, 200°C/400°F/Gas Mark 6, for 20 minutes or until beginning to char slightly. Let the (bell) peppers cool slightly and thinly slice. Arrange in the base of the pastry case, layering with the Mozzarella cheese.

4 Beat the egg and milk and add the basil. Season and pour over the (bell) peppers. Put the tart on a baking tray (cookie sheet) and return to the oven for 20 minutes or until set. Serve hot or cold.

COOK'S TIP

Make sure that the olives are very finely chopped, otherwise they will make holes in the pastry.

Vegetable Biryani

The Biryani originated in the North of India, and was a dish reserved for festivals. The vegetables are marinated in a yogurt-based marinade and cooked in a casserole dish with the rice and onions.

Serves 4

INGREDIENTS

1 large potato, cubed
100 g/3^1/$_2$ oz baby carrots
50 g/1^3/$_4$ oz okra, thickly sliced
2 celery sticks, sliced
75 g/2^3/$_4$ oz baby button mushrooms, halved

1 aubergine (eggplant), halved and sliced
300 ml/^{1}/$_2$ pint/1^1/$_4$ cups natural (unsweetened) yogurt
1 tbsp grated root ginger
2 large onions, grated
4 garlic cloves, crushed

1 tsp turmeric
1 tbsp curry powder
2 tbsp butter
2 onions, sliced
225 g/8 oz/1^1/$_4$ cups basmati rice
chopped coriander (cilantro), to garnish

1 Cook the potato cubes, carrots and okra in a pan of boiling salted water for 7–8 minutes. Drain well and place in a large bowl. Mix with the celery, mushrooms and aubergine (eggplant).

2 Mix the natural (unsweetened) yogurt, ginger, grated onions, garlic, turmeric and curry powder and spoon over the vegetables. Leave to marinate for at least 2 hours.

3 Heat the butter in a frying pan (skillet) and cook the sliced onions for 5–6 minutes until golden brown. Remove a few onions from the pan and reserve for garnishing.

4 Cook the rice in a pan of boiling water for 7 minutes. Drain well.

5 Add the marinated vegetables to the onions and cook for 10 minutes.

6 Put half of the rice in a 2 litre/3^1/$_2$ pint casserole dish. Spoon the vegetables on top and cover with the remaining rice. Cover and cook in a preheated oven, 190°C/375°F/Gas Mark 5, for 20–25 minutes or until the rice is tender.

7 Spoon the biryani on to a serving plate, garnish with the reserved onions and chopped coriander (cilantro) and serve immediately.

Baked Cheese & Tomato Macaroni

*This is a really simple, family dish which is easy
to prepare and cook. Serve with a salad.*

Serves 4

INGREDIENTS

225 g/8 oz/2 cups elbow macaroni
175 g/6 oz/1$^{1}/_{2}$ cups grated
vegetarian cheese
100 g/3$^{1}/_{2}$ oz/1 cup grated Parmesan
cheese
4 tbsp fresh white breadcrumbs

1 tbsp chopped basil
1 tbsp butter or margarine

TOMATO SAUCE:
1 tbsp olive oil
1 shallot, finely chopped

2 garlic cloves, crushed
450 g/1 lb canned chopped tomatoes
1 tbsp chopped basil
salt and pepper

1 To make the tomato sauce, heat the oil in a saucepan and sauté the shallots and garlic for 1 minute. Add the tomatoes, basil, salt and pepper to taste and cook over a medium heat, stirring, for 10 minutes.

2 Meanwhile, cook the macaroni in a pan of boiling salted water for 8 minutes or until just undercooked. Drain.

3 Mix both of the cheeses together.

4 Grease a deep, ovenproof dish. Spoon a third of the tomato sauce into the base of the dish, top with a third of the macaroni and then a third of the cheeses. Season with salt and pepper. Repeat the layers twice.

5 Combine the breadcrumbs and basil and sprinkle over the top. Dot with the butter or margarine and cook in a preheated oven, 190°C/375°F/Gas Mark 5, for 25 minutes or until the dish is golden brown and bubbling. Serve.

COOK'S TIP

Use other pasta shapes, such as penne, if you have them to hand, instead of the macaroni.

Chick-pea (Garbanzo Bean) & Vegetable Casserole

This hearty dish is best served with warm crusty bread to mop up the delicious juices.

Serves 4

INGREDIENTS

1 tbsp olive oil
1 red onion, halved and sliced
3 garlic cloves, crushed
225 g/8 oz spinach
1 fennel bulb, cut into eight
1 red (bell) pepper, cubed

1 tbsp plain (all-purpose) flour
450 ml/^{3}/$_4$ pint/3^3/$_4$ cups vegetable stock
85 ml/3 fl oz/6 tbsp dry white wine
400 g/14 oz can chick-peas (garbanzo beans), drained

1 bay leaf
1 tsp ground coriander
^{1}/$_2$ tsp paprika
salt and pepper
fennel fronds, to garnish

1 Heat the olive oil in a large flameproof casserole dish and sauté the onion and garlic for 1 minute, stirring. Add the spinach and cook for 4 minutes or until wilted.

2 Add the fennel and (bell) pepper and cook for 2 minutes, stirring.

3 Stir in the flour and cook for 1 minute.

4 Add the stock, wine, chick-peas (garbanzo beans), bay leaf, coriander and paprika, cover and cook for 30 minutes. Season to taste, garnish with fennel fronds and serve immediately.

VARIATION

Replace the coriander with nutmeg, if you prefer, as it works particularly well with spinach.

COOK'S TIP

Use other canned pulses or mixed beans instead of the chick-peas (garbanzo beans), if you prefer.

Sweet & Sour Vegetables & Tofu (Bean Curd)

Serve this dish with plain noodles or fluffy white rice for a filling, Oriental meal.

Serves 4

INGREDIENTS

1 tbsp peanut oil
2 garlic cloves, crushed
1 tsp grated root ginger
50 g/1³/₄ oz baby corn cobs
50 g/1³/₄ oz mangetout (snow peas)
1 carrot, cut into matchsticks

1 green (bell) pepper, cut into matchsticks
8 spring onions (scallions), trimmed
50 g/1³/₄ oz canned bamboo shoots
225 g/8 oz marinated firm tofu (bean curd), cubed
2 tbsp dry sherry

2 tbsp rice vinegar
2 tbsp clear honey
1 tbsp light soy sauce
150 ml/¹/₄ pint/²/₃ cup vegetable stock
1 tbsp cornflour (cornstarch)

1 Heat the oil in a preheated wok until almost smoking.

2 Add the garlic and grated root ginger and cook for 30 seconds, stirring frequently.

3 Add the baby corn cobs, mangetout (snow peas), carrot and (bell) pepper and stir-fry for about 5 minutes or until the vegetables are tender.

4 Add the spring onions (scallions), bamboo shoots and tofu (bean curd) and cook for a further 2 minutes.

5 Stir in the sherry, rice vinegar, honey, soy sauce, vegetable stock and cornflour (cornstarch) and bring to the boil. Reduce the heat and simmer for 2 minutes. Transfer to serving dishes and serve immediately.

VARIATION

You can replace any of the vegetables in this dish with others of your choice. For a colourful, attractive stir-fry, select vegetables with bright, contrasting colours.

Spicy Potato & Lemon Casserole

*This is based on a Moroccan dish in which potatoes are spiced
with coriander (cilantro) and cumin and cooked in a lemon sauce.*

Serves 4

INGREDIENTS

100 ml/3^1/$_2$ fl oz/^{1}/$_2$ cup olive oil
2 red onions, cut into eight
3 garlic cloves, crushed
2 tsp ground cumin
2 tsp ground coriander

pinch of cayenne pepper
1 carrot, thickly sliced
2 small turnips, quartered
1 courgette (zucchini), sliced
450 g/1 lb potatoes, thickly sliced

juice and rind of 2 large lemons
300 ml/^{1}/$_2$ pint/1^1/$_4$ cups vegetable
  stock
2 tbsp chopped coriander (cilantro)
salt and pepper

1 Heat the olive oil in a
flameproof casserole.

2 Add the red onion and sauté
for 3 minutes, stirring.

3 Add the garlic and cook for
30 seconds. Mix in the spices
and cook for 1 minute, stirring.

4 Add the carrot, turnips,
courgette (zucchini) and
potatoes and stir to coat in the oil.

5 Add the lemon juice and
rind, stock and salt and

pepper to taste, cover and cook
over a medium heat for 20–30
minutes, stirring occasionally.

6 Remove the lid, sprinkle in
the coriander (cilantro) and
stir well. Serve immediately.

COOK'S TIP

*A selection of spices and
herbs is important for
adding variety to your
cooking – add to your range
each time you try a new recipe.*

COOK'S TIP

*Check the vegetables whilst cooking
as they may begin to stick to the
pan. Add a little more boiling water
or stock if necessary.*

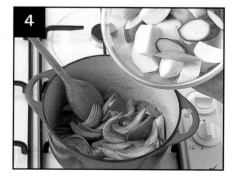

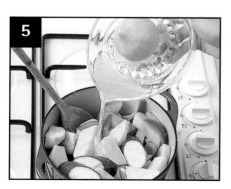

Vegetable Cannelloni

This dish is made with prepared cannelloni tubes,
but may also be made by rolling ready-bought lasagne sheets.

Serves 4

INGREDIENTS

1 aubergine (eggplant)
125 ml/4 fl oz/^{1}/$_2$ cup olive oil
225 g/8 oz spinach
2 garlic cloves, crushed
1 tsp ground cumin
75 g/2^3/$_4$ oz/1 cup mushrooms,
   chopped

12 cannelloni tubes
salt and pepper

TOMATO SAUCE:
1 tbsp olive oil
1 onion, chopped
2 garlic cloves, crushed

2 x 400 g/14 oz cans chopped
   tomatoes
1 tsp caster (superfine) sugar
2 tbsp chopped basil
50 g/1^3/$_4$ oz/^{1}/$_2$ cup Mozzarella,
   sliced

1 Cut the aubergine (eggplant) into small dice.

2 Heat the oil in a frying pan (skillet) and cook the aubergine (eggplant) for 2–3 minutes.

3 Add the spinach, garlic, cumin and mushrooms. Season and cook for 2–3 minutes, stirring. Spoon the mixture into the cannelloni tubes and place in an ovenproof dish in a single layer.

4 To make the sauce, heat the olive oil in a saucepan and sauté the onion and garlic for 1 minute. Add the tomatoes, caster (superfine) sugar and chopped basil and bring to the boil. Reduce the heat and simmer for about 5 minutes. Pour the sauce over the cannelloni tubes.

5 Arrange the sliced Mozzarella on top of the sauce and cook in a preheated oven, 190°C/375°F/ Gas Mark 5, for 30 minutes or until the cheese is bubbling and golden brown. Serve immediately.

COOK'S TIP

You can prepare the tomato sauce in advance and store it in the refrigerator for up to 24 hours.

Cauliflower Bake

*The red of the tomatoes is a great contrast to the cauliflower and herbs,
making this dish appealing to both the eye and the palate.*

Serves 4

INGREDIENTS

450 g/1 lb cauliflower, broken into
  florets
2 large potatoes, cubed
100 g/3¹/₂ oz cherry tomatoes

SAUCE:
25 g/1 oz/2 tbsp butter or vegetarian
  margarine
1 leek, sliced
1 garlic clove, crushed
25 g/1 oz/3 tbsp plain (all-purpose)
  flour
300 ml/¹/₂ pint/1¹/₄ cups milk

75 g/2³/₄ oz/³/₄ cup mixed grated
  cheese, such as vegetarian
  Cheddar, Parmesan and Gruyère
¹/₂ tsp paprika
2 tbsp chopped flat-leaf parsley
salt and pepper
chopped fresh parsley, to garnish

1 Cook the cauliflower in a saucepan of boiling water for 10 minutes. Drain well and reserve. Meanwhile, cook the potatoes in a pan of boiling water for 10 minutes, drain and reserve.

2 To make the sauce, melt the butter or margarine in a saucepan and sauté the leek and garlic for 1 minute. Add the flour and cook for 1 minute. Remove the pan from the heat and

gradually stir in the milk, 50 g/1³/₄ oz/¹/₂ cup of the cheese, the paprika and parsley. Return the pan to the heat and bring to the boil, stirring. Season with salt and pepper to taste.

3 Spoon the cauliflower into a deep ovenproof dish. Add the cherry tomatoes and top with the potatoes. Pour the sauce over the potatoes and sprinkle on the remaining cheese.

4 Cook in a preheated oven, 180°C/350°F/Gas Mark 4, for 20 minutes or until the vegetables are cooked through and the cheese is golden brown and bubbling. Garnish and serve immediately.

VARIATION

This dish could be made with broccoli instead of the cauliflower as an alternative.

Leek & Herb Soufflé

Hot soufflés look very impressive if served as soon as they come out of the oven, otherwise they will sink quite quickly.

Serves 4

INGREDIENTS

350 g/12 oz baby leeks
1 tbsp olive oil
125 ml/4 fl oz/^{1}/$_2$ cup vegetable stock

50 g/1^3/$_4$ oz/^{1}/$_2$ cup walnuts
2 eggs, separated
2 tbsp chopped mixed herbs

2 tbsp natural (unsweetened) yogurt
salt and pepper

1 Using a sharp knife, chop the leeks finely.

2 Heat the oil in a frying pan (skillet) and sauté the leeks for 2–3 minutes.

3 Add the stock to the pan and cook over a gentle heat for a further 5 minutes.

4 Place the walnuts in a food processor and blend until finely chopped.

5 Add the leek mixture to the nuts and blend to form a purée. Transfer to a mixing bowl.

6 Combine the egg yolks, herbs and yogurt and pour into the leek purée. Season with salt and pepper to taste and mix well.

7 In a separate mixing bowl, whisk the egg whites until firm peaks form.

8 Fold the egg whites into the leek mixture. Spoon the mixture into a lightly greased 900 ml/1½ pint ramekin dish and place on a warmed baking tray (cookie sheet).

9 Cook in a preheated oven, 180°C/350°F/Gas Mark 4, for 35–40 minutes or until set. Serve the soufflé immediately.

COOK'S TIP

Placing the ramekin on to a warm baking tray (cookie sheet) helps to cook the soufflé from the bottom, thus aiding its cooking.

Artichoke & Cheese Tart

Artichoke hearts are delicious to eat, being very delicate in flavour and appearance. They are ideal for cooking in a cheese-flavoured pastry case.

Serves 8

INGREDIENTS

175 g/6 oz/1¼ cups wholemeal (whole wheat) flour
2 garlic cloves, crushed
75 g/2¾ oz/6 tbsp butter or vegetarian margarine
salt and pepper

FILLING:
2 tbsp olive oil
1 red onion, halved and sliced
10 canned or fresh artichoke hearts
100 g/3½ oz/1 cup vegetarian Cheddar, grated

50 g/1¾ oz/½ cup Gorgonzola cheese, crumbled
2 eggs, beaten
1 tbsp chopped fresh rosemary
150 ml/¼ pint/⅔ cup milk

1 To make the pastry, sieve the flour into a mixing bowl, add a pinch of salt and the garlic. Rub in the butter until the mixture resembles breadcrumbs. Stir in 3 tablespoons of water and bring the mixture together to form a dough.

2 Roll the pastry out on a lightly floured surface to fit a 20cm/8 inch flan tin (pan). Prick the pastry with a fork.

3 Heat the oil in a frying pan (skillet) and sauté the onion for 3 minutes. Add the artichoke hearts and cook for a further 2 minutes.

4 Mix the cheeses with the beaten eggs, rosemary and milk. Stir in the drained artichoke mixture and season to taste.

5 Spoon the artichoke and cheese mixture into the pastry case and cook in a preheated oven, 200°C/400°F/Gas Mark 6, for 25 minutes or until cooked and set. Serve the flan hot or cold.

COOK'S TIP

Gently press the centre of the flan with your fingertip to test if it is cooked through. It should feel fairly firm, but not solid. If overcooked the flan will begin to 'weep'.

Tagliatelle with Courgette (Zucchini) Sauce

This is a really fresh tasting dish which is ideal with a crisp white wine and some crusty bread.

Serves 4

INGREDIENTS

650 g/1 lb 7 oz courgettes (zucchini)
6 tbsp olive oil
3 garlic cloves, crushed
3 tbsp chopped basil
2 red chillies, sliced

juice of 1 large lemon
5 tbsp single (light) cream
4 tbsp grated Parmesan cheese
225 g/8 oz tagliatelle
salt and pepper

1 Using a vegetable peeler, slice the courgettes (zucchini) into thin ribbons.

2 Heat the oil in a frying pan (skillet) and sauté the garlic for 30 seconds.

3 Add the courgettes (zucchini) and cook over a gentle heat, stirring, for 5–7 minutes.

4 Stir in the basil, chillies, lemon juice, single (light) cream and grated Parmesan cheese and season with salt and pepper to taste.

5 Meanwhile, cook the tagliatelle in a large pan of lightly salted boiling water for 10 minutes until 'al dente'. Drain the pasta thoroughly and put in a warm serving bowl.

6 Pile the courgette (zucchini) mixture on top of the pasta. Serve immediately.

VARIATION

Lime juice and zest could be used instead of the lemon as an alternative.

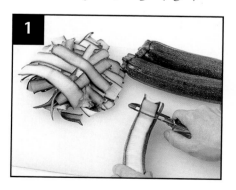

Olive, (Bell) Pepper & Cherry Tomato Pasta

The sweet cherry tomatoes in this recipe add colour and flavour and are complemented by the black olives and (bell) peppers.

Serves 4

INGREDIENTS

225 g/8 oz/2 cups penne
2 tbsp olive oil
2 tbsp butter
2 garlic cloves, crushed
1 green (bell) pepper, thinly sliced

1 yellow (bell) pepper, thinly sliced
16 cherry tomatoes, halved
1 tbsp chopped oregano
125 ml/4 fl oz/^{1}/$_{2}$ cup dry white wine
2 tbsp quartered, pitted black olives

75 g/2^{3}/$_{4}$ oz rocket
salt and pepper
fresh oregano sprigs, to garnish

1 Cook the pasta in a saucepan of boiling salted water for 8–10 minutes or until 'al dente'. Drain thoroughly.

2 Heat the oil and butter in a pan until the butter melts. Sauté the garlic for 30 seconds. Add the (bell) peppers and cook for 3–4 minutes, stirring.

3 Stir in the cherry tomatoes, oregano, wine and olives and cook for 3–4 minutes. Season well

with salt and pepper and stir in the rocket until just wilted.

4 Transfer the pasta to a serving dish, spoon over the sauce and mix well. Garnish and serve.

VARIATION

If rocket is unavailable, spinach makes a good substitute. Follow the same cooking instructions as for rocket.

COOK'S TIP

Ensure that the saucepan is large enough to prevent the pasta from sticking together during cooking.

Spinach & Pine Kernel (Nut) Pasta

*Use any pasta shapes that you have for this recipe,
the tricolore pasta being visually the best to use.*

Serves 4

INGREDIENTS

225 g/8 oz pasta shapes or spaghetti
125 ml/4 fl oz/¹/₂ cup olive oil
2 garlic cloves, crushed
1 onion, quartered and sliced
3 large flat mushrooms, sliced

225 g/8 oz spinach
2 tbsp pine kernels (nuts)
85 ml/3 fl oz/6 tbsp dry white wine
salt and pepper
Parmesan shavings, to garnish

1 Cook the pasta in a saucepan of boiling salted water for 8–10 minutes or until 'al dente'. Drain well.

2 Meanwhile, heat the oil in a large saucepan and sauté the garlic and onion for 1 minute.

3 Add the sliced mushrooms and cook for 2 minutes, stirring occasionally.

4 Add the spinach and cook for 4–5 minutes or until the spinach has wilted.

5 Stir in the pine kernels (nuts) and wine, season well and cook for 1 minute.

6 Transfer the pasta to a warm serving bowl and toss the sauce into it, mixing well. Garnish with shavings of Parmesan cheese and serve.

COOK'S TIP

'Al dente' means that the pasta should be tender but still have a bite to it.

COOK'S TIP

Freshly grate a little nutmeg over the dish for extra flavour as it is particularly good with spinach.

Tofu (Bean Curd) & Vegetable Stir-Fry

*This is a quick dish to prepare, making it ideal as a mid-week supper dish,
after a busy day at work!*

Serves 4

INGREDIENTS

175 g/6 oz/1¹/₄ cups potatoes, cubed
1 tbsp olive oil
1 red onion, sliced
225 g/8 oz firm tofu (bean curd),
  diced
2 courgettes (zucchini), diced

8 canned artichoke hearts, halved
150 ml/¹/₄ pint/²/₃ cup passata
  (sieved tomatoes)
1 tsp caster (superfine) sugar

2 tbsp chopped basil
salt and pepper

1 Cook the potatoes in a saucepan of boiling water for 10 minutes. Drain thoroughly and set aside until required.

2 Heat the oil in a large frying pan (skillet) and sauté the red onion for 2 minutes until the onion has softened, stirring.

3 Stir in the tofu (bean curd) and courgettes (zucchini) and cook for 3–4 minutes until they begin to brown slightly. Add the potatoes, stirring to mix.

4 Stir in the artichoke hearts, passata (sieved tomatoes), sugar and basil, season with salt and pepper and cook for a further 5 minutes, stirring well. Transfer the stir-fry to serving dishes and serve immediately.

VARIATION

Aubergines (eggplants) could be used instead of the courgettes (zucchini), if preferred.

COOK'S TIP

Canned artichoke hearts should be drained thoroughly and rinsed before use because they often have salt added.

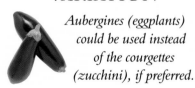

Cantonese Garden Vegetable Stir-Fry

This dish tastes as fresh as it looks. Try to get hold of baby vegetables as they look and taste so much better in this dish.

Serves 4

INGREDIENTS

2 tbsp peanut oil
1 tsp Chinese five-spice powder
75 g/2³/₄ oz baby carrots, halved
2 celery sticks, sliced
2 baby leeks, sliced
50 g/1³/₄ oz mangetout (snow peas)

4 baby courgettes (zucchini), halved lengthwise
8 baby corn cobs
225 g/8 oz firm marinated tofu (bean curd), cubed
4 tbsp fresh orange juice

1 tbsp clear honey
celery leaves and orange zest, to garnish
cooked rice or noodles, to serve

1 Heat the oil in a preheated wok until almost smoking. Add the Chinese five-spice powder, carrots, celery, leeks, mangetout (snow peas), courgettes (zucchini) and corn cobs and stir-fry for 3–4 minutes.

2 Add the tofu (bean curd) and cook for a further 2 minutes, stirring.

3 Stir in the orange juice and honey, reduce the heat and cook for 1–2 minutes.

4 Transfer the stir-fry to a serving dish, garnish with celery leaves and orange zest and serve with rice or noodles.

COOK'S TIP

Chinese five-spice powder is a mixture of fennel, star anise, cinnamon bark, cloves and Szechuan pepper. It is very pungent so should be used sparingly. If kept in an airtight container, it will keep indefinitely.

VARIATION

Lemon juice would be just as delicious as the orange juice in this recipe, but use 3 tablespoons instead of 4 tablespoons.

Risotto Verde

*Risotto is an Italian dish which is easy to make and uses arborio rice,
onion and garlic as a base for a range of savoury recipes.*

Serves 4

INGREDIENTS

1.75 litres/3 pints/7^1/2 cups vegetable stock
2 tbsp olive oil
2 garlic cloves, crushed
2 leeks, shredded
225 g/8 oz/1^1/4 cups arborio rice

300 ml/^{1}/2 pint/1^1/4 cups dry white wine
4 tbsp chopped mixed herbs
225 g/8 oz baby spinach
3 tbsp natural (unsweetened) yogurt
salt and pepper

shredded leek, to garnish

1 Pour the stock into a large saucepan and bring to the boil. Reduce the heat to a simmer.

2 Meanwhile, heat the oil in a separate pan and sauté the garlic and leeks for 2–3 minutes until softened.

3 Stir in the rice and cook for 2 minutes, stirring until well coated.

4 Pour in half of the wine and a little of the hot stock. Cook over a gentle heat until all of the liquid has been absorbed. Add the remaining stock and wine and cook over a low heat for 25 minutes or until the rice is creamy.

5 Stir in the chopped mixed herbs and baby spinach, season well with salt and pepper and cook for 2 minutes.

6 Stir in the natural (unsweetened) yogurt, garnish with the shredded leek and serve immediately.

COOK'S TIP

Do not hurry the process of cooking the risotto as the rice must absorb the liquid slowly in order for it to reach the correct consistency.

Baked Pasta in Tomato Sauce

This pasta dish is baked in a pudding basin and cut into slices for serving.
It looks and tastes terrific and is perfect when you want to impress.

Serves 8

INGREDIENTS

100 g/3^1/2 oz/1 cup pasta shapes,
  such as penne or casareccia
1 tbsp olive oil
1 leek, chopped
3 garlic cloves, crushed
1 green (bell) pepper, chopped
400 g/14 oz can chopped tomatoes

2 tbsp chopped, pitted black olives
2 eggs, beaten
1 tbsp chopped basil

TOMATO SAUCE:
1 tbsp olive oil
1 onion, chopped

225 g/8 oz can chopped tomatoes
1 tsp caster (superfine) sugar
2 tbsp tomato purée (paste)
150 ml/^{1}/4 pint/^{2}/3 cup vegetable
  stock
salt and pepper

1 Cook the pasta in a saucepan of boiling salted water for 8 minutes. Drain thoroughly.

2 Meanwhile, heat the oil in a saucepan and sauté the leek and garlic for 2 minutes, stirring. Add the (bell) pepper, tomatoes and olives and cook for a further 5 minutes.

3 Remove the pan from the heat and stir in the pasta, beaten eggs and basil. Season well, and spoon into a lightly greased 1 litre/2 pint ovenproof pudding basin.

4 Place the pudding basin in a roasting tin (pan) and half-fill the tin (pan) with boiling water. Cover and cook in a preheated oven, 180°C/350°F/Gas Mark 6, for 40 minutes until set.

5 To make the sauce, heat the oil in a pan and sauté the onion for 2 minutes. Add the remaining ingredients and cook for 10 minutes. Put the sauce in a food processor or blender and blend until smooth. Return to a clean saucepan and heat until hot.

6 Turn the pasta out of the pudding basin on to a warm plate. Slice and serve with the tomato sauce.

Spaghetti with Pear & Walnut Sauce

*This is quite an unusual combination of ingredients in a savoury dish,
but is absolutely wonderful tossed into a fine pasta such as spaghetti.*

Serves 4

INGREDIENTS

225 g/8 oz spaghetti
2 small ripe pears, peeled and sliced
150 ml/$^1/_4$ pint/$^2/_3$ cup vegetable
  stock
85 ml/3 fl oz/6 tbsp dry white wine
2 tbsp butter

1 tbsp olive oil
1 red onion, quartered and sliced
1 garlic clove, crushed
50 g/1$^3/_4$ oz/$^1/_2$ cup walnut halves
2 tbsp chopped oregano
1 tbsp lemon juice

75 g/2$^3/_4$ oz/$^3/_4$ cup dolcelatte cheese
salt and pepper
fresh oregano sprigs, to garnish

1 Cook the pasta in a saucepan of boiling salted water for 8–10 minutes or until 'al dente'. Drain thoroughly and keep warm until required.

2 Meanwhile, place the pears in a pan and pour over the stock and wine. Poach the pears over a gentle heat for 10 minutes. Drain and reserve the cooking liquid and pears.

3 Heat the butter and oil in a saucepan until the butter melts, then sauté the onion and garlic for 2–3 minutes, stirring.

4 Add the walnuts, oregano and lemon juice, stirring.

5 Stir in the reserved pears with 4 tablespoons of the poaching liquid.

6 Crumble the dolcelatte cheese into the pan and cook over a gentle heat, stirring occasionally, for 1–2 minutes or until the cheese just begins to melt. Season the sauce with salt and pepper to taste.

7 Toss the pasta into the sauce, garnish and serve.

COOK'S TIP

You can use any good-flavoured blue cheese for this dish. Other varieties to try are Roquefort, which has a very strong flavour, Gorgonzola or Stilton.

Side Dishes

If you are running short of ideas for interesting side dishes to serve with your main meals, these recipes will be a welcome inspiration. An ideal accompaniment complements the main dish both visually and nutritionally. Many main dishes will be rich in protein, therefore the side dishes in this chapter have been created to be a little lighter in texture but still packed full of colour and flavour. They have been cooked in many different ways – there are bakes, fries, steamed vegetables and braises, all of which are perfect accompaniments for all occasions.

This chapter also contains a selection of delicious salads which are bursting with flavour and colour. Make one of these salads to accompany your main meal, or make larger portions to serve alone. Choose the right salad to serve with your main meal – make sure that the flavours and textures complement rather than clash with one another. The secret of a successful salad relies on one important aspect: the freshness of the ingredients. Try some of of the ideas in this chapter and discover some sensational side dishes to add to your repertoire.

Cheese & Potato Layer Bake

*This really is a great side dish, perfect for serving
with main meals cooked in the oven.*

Serves 4

INGREDIENTS

450 g/1 lb potatoes
1 leek, sliced
3 garlic cloves, crushed
50 g/1³/₄ oz/¹/₂ cup Cheddar, grated
50 g/1³/₄ oz/¹/₂ cup Mozzarella,
   grated

25 g/1 oz/¹/₄ cup Parmesan cheese,
   grated
2 tbsp chopped parsley
150 ml/¹/₄ pint/²/₃ cup single (light)
   cream
150 ml/¹/₄ pint/²/₃ cup milk

salt and pepper
freshly chopped flat-leaf parsley,
   to garnish

1 Cook the potatoes in a saucepan of boiling salted water for 10 minutes. Drain well.

2 Cut the potatoes into thin slices. Arrange a layer of potatoes in the base of an ovenproof dish. Layer with a little of the leek, garlic, cheeses and parsley. Season well.

3 Repeat the layers until all of the ingredients have been used, finishing with a layer of cheese on top.

4 Mix the cream and milk together, season with salt and pepper to taste and pour over the potato layers.

5 Cook in a preheated oven, 160°C/325°F/Gas Mark 3, for 1–1¼ hours or until the cheese is golden brown and bubbling and the potatoes are cooked through.

6 Garnish with freshly chopped flat-leaf parsley and serve immediately.

COOK'S TIP

Stir the vegetables occasionally during the 30 minutes cooking time to prevent them sticking to the bottom of the pan. If the liquid has not evaporated by the end of the cooking time, remove the lid and boil rapidly until the dish is dry.

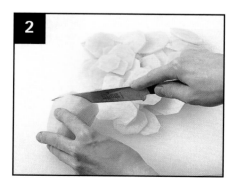

Cauliflower & Broccoli with Herb Sauce

Whole baby cauliflowers are used in this recipe. Try to find them if you can, if not use large bunches of florets.

Serves 4

INGREDIENTS

2 baby cauliflowers
225 g/8 oz broccoli
salt and pepper

SAUCE:
8 tbsp olive oil
4 tbsp butter or vegetarian margarine
2 tsp grated root ginger

juice and rind of 2 lemons
5 tbsp chopped coriander (cilantro)
5 tbsp grated Cheddar

1 Using a sharp knife, cut the cauliflowers in half and the broccoli into very large florets.

2 Cook the cauliflower and broccoli in a saucepan of boiling salted water for 10 minutes. Drain well, transfer to a shallow ovenproof dish and keep warm until required.

3 To make the sauce, put the oil and butter or vegetarian margarine in a pan and heat gently until the butter melts. Add the grated root ginger, lemon juice, lemon rind and coriander (cilantro) and simmer for 2–3 minutes, stirring occasionally.

4 Season the sauce with salt and pepper to taste, then pour over the vegetables in the dish and sprinkle the cheese on top.

5 Cook under a preheated hot grill (broiler) for 2–3 minutes or until the cheese is bubbling and golden. Leave to cool for 1–2 minutes and then serve.

VARIATION

Lime or orange could be used instead of the lemon for a fruity and refreshing sauce.

Indian Spiced Potatoes & Spinach

This is a classic Indian accompaniment for
curries or plainer main vegetable dishes.

Serves 4

INGREDIENTS

3 tbsp vegetable oil
1 red onion, sliced
2 garlic cloves, crushed
$1/2$ tsp chilli powder
2 tsp ground coriander

1 tsp ground cumin
150 ml/$1/4$ pint/$2/3$ cup vegetable
  stock
300 g/$10^{1}/2$ oz/$2/3$ cup potatoes,
  cubed

450 g/1 lb baby spinach
1 red chilli, sliced
salt and pepper

1 Heat the oil in a frying pan (skillet) and sauté the onion and garlic for 2–3 minutes, stirring occasionally.

2 Stir in the chilli powder, ground coriander and cumin and cook for a further 30 seconds.

3 Add the vegetable stock, potato and spinach and bring to the boil. Reduce the heat, cover the frying pan (skillet) and simmer for about 10 minutes or until the potatoes are cooked through.

4 Uncover, season to taste, add the chilli and cook for a further 2–3 minutes. Serve.

COOK'S TIP

Be very careful when handling chillies– never touch your face or eyes as the juices can be very painful and always wash your hands thoroughly after preparing chillies. The seeds are the hottest part of the chilli but have less flavour, so these are usually removed before use.

VARIATION

Add other vegetables, such as chopped tomatoes, for colour and flavour.

Side Dishes

Steamed Vegetables with Vermouth

Serve these vegetables in their paper parcels to retain the juices.
The result is truly delicious.

Serves 4

INGREDIENTS

1 carrot, cut into batons
1 fennel bulb, sliced
100 g/3¹/₂ oz courgettes
   (zucchini), sliced
1 red (bell) pepper, sliced
4 small onions, halved

8 tbsp vermouth
4 tbsp lime juice
zest of 1 lime
pinch of paprika
4 sprigs tarragon
salt and pepper

fresh tarragon sprigs, to garnish

1 Place all of the vegetables in a large bowl and mix well.

2 Cut 4 large squares of baking parchment and place a quarter of the vegetables in the centre of each. Bring the sides of the paper up and pinch together to make an open parcel.

3 Mix together the vermouth, lime juice, lime zest and paprika and pour a quarter of the mixture into each parcel. Season with salt and pepper and add a

tarragon sprig to each. Pinch the tops of the parcels together to seal.

4 Place the parcels in a steamer, cover and cook for 15–20 minutes or until the vegetables are tender. Garnish and serve.

COOK'S TIP

Vermouth is a fortified white wine flavoured with various herbs and spices. It its available in both sweet and dry forms.

COOK'S TIP

Seal the parcels well to prevent them opening during cooking and causing the juices to evaporate.

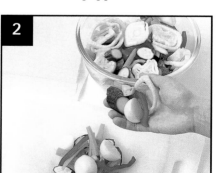

180

Spicy Lentils & Spinach

This is quite a filling dish, and should be served with a light main course.
Green split peas are a type of lentil (legume).

Serves 4

INGREDIENTS

225 g/8 oz/1^1/$_4$ cups green split peas
900 g/2 lb spinach
4 tbsp vegetable oil
1 onion, halved and sliced
1 tsp grated root ginger
1 tsp ground cumin

^{1}/$_2$ tsp chilli powder
^{1}/$_2$ tsp ground coriander
2 garlic cloves, crushed
300 ml/^{1}/$_2$ pint/1^1/$_4$ cups vegetable
  stock
salt and pepper

fresh coriander (cilantro) sprigs and
  lime wedges, to garnish

1 Rinse the peas under cold running water. Transfer to a mixing bowl, cover with cold water and leave to soak for 2 hours. Drain well.

2 Meanwhile, cook the spinach in a large saucepan for 5 minutes until wilted. Drain well and roughly chop.

3 Heat the oil in a large saucepan and sauté the onion, spices and garlic. Sauté for 2–3 minutes, stirring well.

4 Add the lentils and spinach and stir in the stock. Cover and simmer for 10–15 minutes or until the lentils are cooked and the liquid has been absorbed. Season with salt and pepper to taste, garnish and serve.

VARIATION

If you do not have time to soak the green peas, canned puy lentils are a good substitute but remember to drain and rinse them first.

COOK'S TIP

Once the lentils have been added, stir occasionally to prevent them from sticking to the pan.

Beans in Lemon & Herb Sauce

*Use a variety of beans if possible, although this recipe is
perfectly acceptable with just one type of bean.*

Serves 4

INGREDIENTS

900 g/2 lb mixed green beans,
  such as broad (fava) beans,
  French (green) beans, runner beans
65 g/2$^{1}/_{2}$ oz/$^{1}/_{2}$ cup butter or
  vegetarian margarine
4 tsp plain (all-purpose) flour

300 ml/$^{1}/_{2}$ pint/1$^{1}/_{4}$ cups vegetable
  stock
85 ml/3 fl oz dry white wine
6 tbsp single (light) cream
3 tbsp chopped mixed herbs
2 tbsp lemon juice

rind of 1 lemon
salt and pepper

1 Cook the beans in a saucepan of boiling salted water for 10 minutes or until tender. Drain and place in a warm serving dish.

2 Meanwhile, melt the butter in a saucepan. Add the flour and cook for 1 minute. Remove the pan from the heat and gradually stir in the stock and wine. Return the pan to the heat and bring to the boil.

3 Remove the pan from the heat once again and stir in the single (light) cream, mixed herbs, lemon juice and zest. Season with salt and pepper to taste. Pour the sauce over the beans, mixing well. Serve immediately.

VARIATION

*Use lime rind and juice instead of
lemon for an alternative
citrus flavour. Replace the single
(light) cream with natural
(unsweetened) yogurt for a
healthier version of this dish.*

COOK'S TIP

*Use a wide
variety of herbs for
flavour, such as
rosemary, thyme,
tarragon and sage.*

Curried Cauliflower & Spinach

The contrast in colour in this recipe makes it very appealing to the eye, especially as the cauliflower is lightly coloured with yellow turmeric.

Serves 4

INGREDIENTS

1 medium cauliflower
6 tbsp vegetable oil
1 tsp mustard seeds
1 tsp ground cumin
1 tsp garam masala
1 tsp turmeric

2 garlic cloves, crushed
1 onion, halved and sliced
1 green chilli, sliced
450 g/1 lb spinach
85 ml/3 fl oz/6 tbsp vegetable stock
1 tbsp chopped coriander (cilantro)

salt and pepper
coriander (cilantro) sprigs, to garnish

1 Break the cauliflower into small florets.

2 Heat the oil in a deep flameproof casserole dish. Add the mustard seeds and cook until they begin to pop.

3 Stir in the remaining spices, the garlic, onion and chilli and cook for 2–3 minutes, stirring.

4 Add the cauliflower, spinach, vegetable stock, coriander (cilantro) and seasoning and cook over a gentle heat for 15 minutes or until the cauliflower is tender. Uncover the dish and boil for 1 minute to thicken the juices. Garnish and serve.

COOK'S TIP

Mustard seeds are used throughout India and are particularly popular in southern vegetarian cooking. They are fried in oil first to bring out their flavour before the other ingredients are added.

VARIATION

Broccoli may be used instead of the cauliflower, if preferred.

Aubergine (Eggplant) & Courgette (Zucchini) Galette

This is a dish of aubergine (eggplant) and courgettes (zucchini) layered with a quick tomato sauce and melted cheese.

Serves 4

INGREDIENTS

2 large aubergines (eggplants), sliced
4 courgettes (zucchini)
2 x 400 g/14 oz cans
   chopped tomatoes, drained
2 tbsp tomato purée (paste)

2 garlic cloves, crushed
50 ml/2 fl oz/4 tbsp olive oil
1 tsp caster (superfine) sugar
2 tbsp chopped basil
olive oil, for frying

225 g/8 oz Mozzarella cheese, sliced
salt and pepper
fresh basil leaves, to garnish

1 Put the aubergine (eggplant) slices in a colander and sprinkle with salt. Leave to stand for 30 minutes, then rinse well under cold water and drain. Thinly slice the courgettes (zucchini).

2 Meanwhile, put the tomatoes, tomato purée (paste), garlic, olive oil, sugar and chopped basil into a pan and simmer for 20 minutes or until reduced by half. Season well.

3 Heat 2 tablespoons of olive oil in a large frying pan (skillet) and cook the aubergine (eggplant) slices for 2–3 minutes until just beginning to brown. Remove from the pan.

4 Add a further 2 tablespoons of oil to the pan and fry the courgette (zucchini) slices until browned.

5 Lay half of the aubergine (eggplant) slices in the base of

an ovenproof dish. Top with half of the tomato sauce and the courgettes (zucchini) and then half of the Mozzarella.

6 Repeat the layers and bake in a preheated oven, 180°C/350°F/Gas Mark 4, for 45–50 minutes or until the vegetables are tender. Garnish with basil leaves and serve.

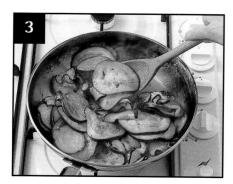

Baked Celery with Cream & Pecans

This dish is topped with breadcrumbs for a crunchy topping, underneath which is hidden a creamy celery and pecan mixture.

Serves 4

INGREDIENTS

1 head of celery
$1/2$ tsp ground cumin
$1/2$ tsp ground coriander
1 garlic clove, crushed
1 red onion, thinly sliced
50 g/$1^3/4$ oz/$1/2$ cup pecan nut halves

150 ml/$1/4$ pint/$2/3$ cup vegetable stock
150 ml/$1/4$ pint/$2/3$ cup single (light) cream
50 g/$1^3/4$ oz fresh wholemeal (whole wheat) breadcrumbs

25 g/1 oz/$1/4$ cup Parmesan cheese, grated
salt and pepper
celery leaves, to garnish

1 Trim the celery and cut into matchsticks. Place the celery in an ovenproof dish with the ground cumin, coriander, garlic, onion and pecan nuts.

2 Mix the stock and cream together and pour over the vegetables. Season with salt and pepper to taste.

3 Mix the breadcrumbs and cheese together and sprinkle over the top to cover the vegetables.

4 Cook in a preheated oven, 200°C/400°F/Gas Mark 6, for 40 minutes or until the vegetables are tender and the top crispy. Garnish with celery leaves and serve at once.

VARIATION

You could use carrots or courgettes (zucchini) instead of the celery, if you prefer.

COOK'S TIP

Once grated, Parmesan cheese quickly loses its 'bite' so it is best to grate only the amount you need for the recipe. Wrap the rest tightly in foil and it will keep for several months in the refrigerator.

Pepperonata

A delicious mixture of (bell) peppers and onions, cooked with tomatoes and herbs for a rich side dish.

Serves 4

INGREDIENTS

4 tbsp olive oil
1 onion, halved and finely sliced
2 red (bell) peppers, cut into strips
2 green (bell) peppers, cut into strips
2 yellow (bell) peppers, cut into strips
2 garlic cloves, crushed

2 x 400 g/14 oz cans chopped
  tomatoes, drained
2 tbsp chopped coriander (cilantro)
2 tbsp chopped pitted black olives
salt and pepper

1 Heat the oil in a large frying pan (skillet). Add the onion and sauté for 5 minutes, stirring until just beginning to colour.

2 Add the (bell) peppers and garlic to the pan and cook for a further 3–4 minutes.

3 Stir in the tomatoes and coriander (cilantro) and season with salt and pepper. Cover the pan and cook the vegetables gently for about 30 minutes or until the mixture is dry.

4 Stir in the pitted black olives and serve the pepperonata immediately.

COOK'S TIP

Stir the vegetables occasionally during the 30 minutes cooking time to prevent them sticking to the bottom of the pan. If the liquid has not evaporated by the end of the cooking time, remove the lid and boil rapidly until the dish is dry.

VARIATION

If you don't like the distinctive flavour of fresh coriander (cilantro), you can substitute it with 2 tbsp chopped fresh flat-leaf parsley. Use green olives instead of black ones, if you prefer.

Soufflèd Cheesy Potato Fries

These small potato chunks are mixed in a creamy cheese sauce and fried in oil until deliciously golden brown.

Serves 4

INGREDIENTS

900 g/2 lb potatoes, cut into chunks
150 ml/^{1}/4 pint/^{2}/3 cup double (heavy) cream
75 g/2^3/4 oz/^{3}/4 cup Gruyère cheese, grated

pinch of cayenne pepper
2 egg whites
oil, for deep-frying
salt and pepper

chopped flat-leaf parsley and grated vegetarian cheese, to garnish

1 Cook the potatoes in a saucepan of boiling salted water for 10 minutes. Drain well and pat dry with absorbent paper towels. Set aside until required.

2 Mix the double (heavy) cream and Gruyère cheese in a large bowl. Stir in the cayenne pepper and season with salt and pepper to taste.

3 Whisk the egg whites until stiff peaks form. Fold into the cheese mixture until fully incorporated.

4 Add the cooked potatoes, turning to coat thoroughly in the mixture.

5 Heat the oil for deep-frying to 180°C/350°F or until a cube of bread browns in 30 seconds. Remove the potatoes from the cheese mixture with a slotted spoon and cook in the oil, in batches, for 3–4 minutes or until golden.

6 Transfer the potatoes to a serving dish and garnish with parsley and grated cheese. Serve.

VARIATION

Add other flavourings, such as grated nutmeg or curry powder, to the cream and cheese.

Bulgur Pilau

Bulgur wheat is very easy to use and is a delicious alternative to rice, having a distinctive nutty flavour.

Serves 4

INGREDIENTS

75 g/2³/4 oz/6 tbsp butter or
  vegetarian margarine
1 red onion, halved and sliced
2 garlic cloves, crushed
350 g/12 oz/2 cups bulgur wheat
175 g/6 oz tomatoes, seeded
  and chopped

50 g/1³/4 oz baby corn cobs,
  halved lengthwise
75 g/2³/4 oz small broccoli florets
850 ml/1¹/2 pints/3³/4 cups vegetable
  stock
2 tbsp clear honey
50 g/1³/4 oz sultanas (golden raisins)

50 g/1³/4 oz pine kernels (nuts)
¹/2 tsp ground cinnamon
¹/2 tsp ground cumin
salt and pepper
sliced spring onions (scallions),
  to garnish

1 Melt the butter or margarine in a large flameproof casserole dish.

2 Add the onion and garlic and sauté for 2–3 minutes, stirring occasionally.

3 Add the bulgur wheat, tomatoes, corn cobs, broccoli and stock and bring to the boil. Reduce the heat, cover and cook for 15–20 minutes, stirring occasionally.

4 Stir in the honey, sultanas (golden raisins), pine kernels (nuts), ground cinnamon, cumin and salt and pepper to taste, mixing well. Remove the casserole from the heat, cover and leave for 10 minutes.

5 Spoon the bulgur pilau into a warm serving dish.

6 Garnish the bulgur pilau with sliced spring onions (scallions) and serve immediately.

COOK'S TIP

The dish is left to stand for 10 minutes in order for the bulgur to finish cooking and the flavours to mingle.

Pesto Potatoes

Pesto sauce is more commonly used as a pasta sauce but is delicious served over potatoes as well.

Serves 4

INGREDIENTS

900 g/2 lb small new potatoes
75 g/2³/₄ oz fresh basil
2 tbsp pine kernels (nuts)
3 garlic cloves, crushed
100 ml/3¹/₂ fl oz/¹/₂ cup olive oil

75 g/2³/₄ oz/³/₄ cup freshly grated
Parmesan cheese and Pecorino
cheese, mixed

salt and pepper
fresh basil sprigs, to garnish

1 Cook the potatoes in a saucepan of boiling salted water for 15 minutes or until tender. Drain well, transfer to a warm serving dish and keep warm until required.

2 Meanwhile, put the basil, pine kernels (nuts), garlic and a little salt and pepper to taste in a food processor. Blend for 30 seconds, adding the oil gradually, until smooth.

3 Remove the mixture from the food processor and place in a mixing bowl. Stir in the grated Parmesan and Pecorino cheeses.

4 Spoon the pesto sauce over the potatoes and mix well. Garnish with fresh basil sprigs and serve immediately.

COOK'S TIP

Store this pesto sauce in an airtight container for up to a week in the refrigerator. It can also be frozen (before adding the cheeses) for several months.

COOK'S TIP

This sauce would also make a great dressing for a crisp green salad.

Carrot, Orange & Poppy Seed Bake

The poppy seeds add texture and flavour to this recipe,
and counteract the slightly sweet flavour of the carrots.

Serves 4

INGREDIENTS

675 g/1 lb 8 oz carrots, cut
   into thin strips
1 leek, sliced
300 ml/$\frac{1}{2}$ pint/1$\frac{1}{4}$ cups fresh
   orange juice
2 tbsp clear honey

1 garlic clove, crushed
1 tsp mixed spice
2 tsp chopped thyme
1 tbsp poppy seeds

salt and pepper
fresh thyme sprigs and orange
   rind, to garnish

1 Cook the carrots and leek in a saucepan of boiling salted water for 5–6 minutes. Drain well and transfer to a shallow baking dish until required.

2 Mix together the orange juice, honey, garlic, mixed spice and thyme and pour the mixture over the vegetables. Add salt and pepper to taste.

3 Cover the baking dish and cook in a preheated oven, 180°C/350°F/Gas Mark 4, for 30 minutes or until the vegetables are tender.

4 Remove the lid and sprinkle with poppy seeds. Garnish with fresh thyme sprigs and orange rind and serve.

VARIATION

If you prefer, use 2 tsp cumin
instead of the mixed spice and omit
the thyme, as cumin works
particularly well with carrots.

COOK'S TIP

Lemon or lime juice could
be used instead of the
orange juice if you
prefer. Garnish with
lemon or lime rind.

Greek Green Beans

This dish contains many Greek flavours such as lemon, garlic, oregano and olives, for a really flavourful recipe.

Serves 4

INGREDIENTS

400 g/14 oz can haricot (navy) beans, drained
1 tbsp olive oil
3 garlic cloves, crushed
425 ml/^{3}/4 pint/2 cups vegetable stock

1 bay leaf
2 sprigs oregano
1 tbsp tomato purée (paste)
juice of 1 lemon
1 small red onion, chopped
25 g/1 oz pitted black olives, halved

salt and pepper

1 Put the haricot (navy) beans in a flameproof casserole dish.

2 Add the olive oil and crushed garlic and cook over a gentle heat, stirring occasionally, for 4–5 minutes.

3 Add the stock, bay leaf, oregano, tomato purée (paste), lemon juice and red onion, cover and simmer for about 1 hour or until the sauce has thickened.

4 Stir in the olives, season with salt and pepper to taste and serve.

VARIATION

You can substitute other canned beans for the haricot (navy) beans – try cannellini or black-eyed beans (peas), or chick-peas (garbanzo beans) instead. Remember to drain and rinse them thoroughly before use as canned beans often have sugar or salt added.

COOK'S TIP

This dish may be made in advance and served cold with crusty bread, if preferred.

Sweet & Sour Aubergines (Eggplants)

This is a dish of Persian origin, not Chinese as it sounds. Aubergines (eggplants) are fried and mixed with tomatoes, mint, sugar and vinegar for a really intense flavour.

Serves 4

INGREDIENTS

2 large aubergines (eggplants)
6 tbsp olive oil
4 garlic cloves, crushed
1 onion, cut into eight
4 large tomatoes,
    seeded and chopped

3 tbsp chopped mint
150 ml/¼ pint/⅔ cup vegetable
    stock
4 tsp brown sugar
2 tbsp red wine vinegar
1 tsp chilli flakes

salt and pepper
fresh mint sprigs, to garnish

1 Using a sharp knife, cut the aubergines (eggplants) into cubes. Put them in a colander, sprinkle with salt and leave to stand for 30 minutes. Rinse thoroughly under cold running water and drain well. This process removes all the bitter juices from the aubergines (eggplants). Pat dry with absorbent paper towels.

2 Heat the oil in a large frying pan (skillet) and sauté the aubergine (eggplant), stirring constantly for 1–2 minutes.

3 Stir in the garlic and onion and cook for a further 2–3 minutes.

4 Stir in the tomatoes, mint and stock, cover and cook for 15–20 minutes or until the vegetables are tender.

5 Stir in the brown sugar, red wine vinegar and chilli flakes, season with salt and pepper to taste and cook for 2–3 minutes. Garnish the aubergines with fresh mint sprigs and serve.

COOK'S TIP

Mint is a popular herb in Middle Eastern cooking. It is a useful herb to grow yourself as it can be added to a variety of dishes, particularly salads and vegetable dishes. It can be grown easily in a garden or window box.

Mini Vegetable Puff Pastry Cases

*These are ideal with a more formal meal as they take
a little time to prepare and look really impressive.*

Serves 4

INGREDIENTS

450 g/1 lb puff pastry
1 egg, beaten

FILLING:
225 g/8 oz sweet potato, cubed
100 g/3¹/₂ oz baby asparagus spears
2 tbsp butter or vegetarian margarine
1 leek, sliced

2 small open-cap mushrooms, sliced
1 tsp lime juice
1 tsp chopped thyme
pinch of dried mustard
salt and pepper

1 Cut the pastry into 4 equal pieces. Roll each piece out on a lightly floured surface to form a 12.5 cm/5 inch square. Place on a dampened baking tray (cookie sheet) and score a smaller 7.5 cm/ 2.5 inch square inside.

2 Brush with beaten egg and cook in a preheated oven, 200°C/400°F/Gas Mark 6, for 20 minutes or until risen and golden brown.

3 Remove the pastry squares from the oven, then carefully cut out the central square of pastry, lift out and reserve.

4 To make the filling, cook the sweet potato in a saucepan of boiling water for 15 minutes, then drain well. Blanch the asparagus in a saucepan of boiling water for 10 minutes or until tender. Drain and reserve.

5 Melt the butter or margarine in a saucepan and sauté the leek and mushrooms for 2–3 minutes. Add the lime juice, thyme and mustard, season well and stir in the sweet potatoes and asparagus. Spoon into the pastry cases, top with the reserved pastry squares and serve immediately.

COOK'S TIP

*Use a colourful selection
of any vegetables you have at hand
for this recipe.*

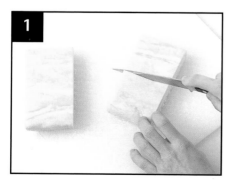

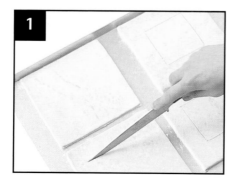

Aubergine (Eggplant) Salad

*This salad uses tahini paste (sesame seed paste) as a flavouring
for the dressing, which complements the aubergine (eggplant).*

Serves 4

INGREDIENTS

1 large aubergine (eggplant)
3 tbsp tahini paste (sesame seed
   paste)
juice and rind of 1 lemon
1 garlic clove, crushed
pinch of paprika

1 tbsp chopped coriander (cilantro)
salt and pepper
Little Gem lettuce leaves

GARNISH:
strips of pimiento
lemon wedges
toasted sesame seeds

1 Cut the aubergine (eggplant) in half, place in a colander and sprinkle with salt. Leave to stand for 30 minutes, rinse under cold running water and drain well. Pat dry with paper towels.

2 Place the aubergine (eggplant) halves, skin-side uppermost, on an oiled baking tray (cookie sheet). Cook in a preheated oven, 230°C/450°F/ Gas Mark 8, for 10–15 minutes. Remove from the oven and allow to cool.

3 Cut the aubergine (eggplant) into cubes and set aside until required. Mix the tahini paste (sesame seed paste), lemon juice and rind, garlic, paprika and coriander (cilantro) together. Season to taste and stir in the aubergine (eggplant).

4 Line a serving dish with lettuce leaves and spoon the aubergine (eggplant) into the centre. Garnish the salad with pimiento slices, lemon wedges and toasted sesame seeds and serve.

COOK'S TIP

Tahini paste (sesame seed paste) is a nutty-flavoured sauce available from most health food shops. It is good served with many Middle Eastern dishes.

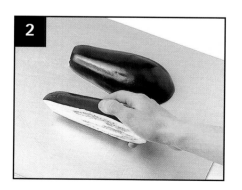

Salad with Garlic & Yogurt Dressing

This is a very quick and refreshing salad using a whole range of colourful ingredients which make it look as good as it tastes.

Serves 4

INGREDIENTS

75 g/2³/₄ oz cucumber,
  cut into sticks
6 spring onions (scallions), halved
2 tomatoes, seeded
  and cut into eight
1 yellow (bell) pepper, cut into strips
2 celery sticks, cut into strips

4 radishes, quartered
75 g/2³/₄ oz rocket
1 tbsp chopped mint, to serve

DRESSING:
2 tbsp lemon juice
1 garlic clove, crushed
150 ml/¹/₄ pint/²/₃ cup natural
  (unsweetened) yogurt
2 tbsp olive oil
salt and pepper

1 Mix the cucumber, spring onions (scallions), tomatoes, (bell) pepper, celery, radishes and rocket together in a large serving bowl.

2 To make the dressing, stir the lemon juice, garlic, natural (unsweetened) yogurt and olive oil together. Season well with salt and pepper.

3 Spoon the dressing over the salad and toss to mix.

4 Sprinkle the salad with chopped mint and serve.

COOK'S TIP

Rocket has a distinct warm, peppery flavour which is ideal in green salads. Once you have grown it in your garden or greenhouse you will always have plenty as it re-seeds all over the place! If rocket is unavailable, lamb's lettuce (corn salad) makes a good substitute.

COOK'S TIP

Do not toss the dressing into the salad until just before serving, otherwise it will turn soggy.

Courgette, Yogurt & Mint Salad

*This salad uses lots of green-coloured ingredients which look and taste
wonderful with the minty yogurt dressing.*

Serves 4

INGREDIENTS

2 courgettes (zucchini), cut into
  sticks
100 g/3$^{1}/_{2}$ oz French (green) beans,
  cut into three
1 green (bell) pepper, cut into strips
2 celery sticks, sliced

1 bunch watercress

DRESSING:
200 ml/7 fl oz/$^{3}/_{4}$ cup natural
  (unsweetened) yogurt
1 garlic clove, crushed
2 tbsp chopped mint
pepper

1 Cook the courgettes (zucchini) and French (green) beans in a saucepan of salted boiling water for 7–8 minutes. Drain and leave to cool completely.

2 Mix the courgettes (zucchini) and French (green) beans with the (bell) pepper, celery and watercress in a large bowl.

3 To make the dressing, mix together the natural (unsweetened) yogurt, garlic and chopped mint in a bowl. Season with pepper to taste.

4 Spoon the dressing on to the salad and serve immediately.

COOK'S TIP

*The salad must be served
as soon as the yogurt dressing has
been added – the dressing will start
to separate if kept for any
length of time.*

COOK'S TIP

*Watercress is available all year
round. Its fresh peppery flavour
makes it a delicious addition
to many salads.*

Bean, Avocado & Tomato Salad

This is a colourful salad with a Mexican theme, using beans, tomatoes and avocado.
The chilli dressing adds a little kick.

Serves 4

INGREDIENTS

lollo rosso lettuce
2 ripe avocados
2 tsp lemon juice
4 medium tomatoes
1 onion

175 g/6 oz/2 cups mixed canned
   beans, drained

DRESSING:
4 tbsp olive oil
drop of chilli oil

2 tbsp garlic wine vinegar
pinch of caster (superfine) sugar
pinch of chilli powder
1 tbsp chopped parsley

1 Line a serving bowl with the lettuce.

2 Using a sharp knife, thinly slice the avocados and sprinkle with the lemon juice.

3 Thinly slice the tomato and onion. Arrange the avocado, tomatoes and onion around the salad bowl, leaving a space in the centre.

4 Spoon the beans into the centre of the salad and whisk the dressing ingredients together. Pour the dressing over the salad and serve.

COOK'S TIP

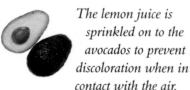

The lemon juice is sprinkled on to the avocados to prevent discoloration when in contact with the air. For this reason the salad should be prepared, assembled and served quite quickly.

COOK'S TIP

Instead of whisking the dressing, place all the ingredients in a screw-top jar and shake vigorously. Any leftover dressing can then be kept and stored in the same jar.

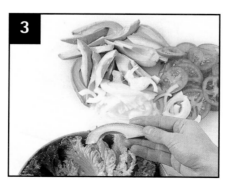

Gado Gado

This is a very well known Indonesian salad of mixed vegetables with a peanut dressing.

Serves 4

INGREDIENTS

100 g/3¹/2 oz/1 cup white cabbage, shredded
100 g/3¹/2 oz French (green) beans, cut into 3
100 g/3¹/2 oz carrots, cut into matchsticks
100 g/3¹/2 oz cauliflower florets

100 g/3¹/2 oz bean sprouts

DRESSING:
100 ml/3¹/2 fl oz/¹/2 cup vegetable oil
100 g/3¹/2 oz/1 cup unsalted peanuts
2 garlic cloves, crushed
1 small onion, finely chopped

¹/2 tsp chilli powder
¹/3 tsp light brown sugar
425 ml/³/4 pint/2 cups water
juice of ¹/2 lemon
salt
sliced spring onions (scallions), to garnish

1 Cook the vegetables separately in a saucepan of salted boiling water for 4–5 minutes, drain well and chill.

2 To make the dressing, heat the oil in a frying pan (skillet) and fry the peanuts for 3–4 minutes, turning.

3 Remove from the pan with a slotted spoon and leave to drain on absorbent paper towels. Grind the peanuts in a blender or crush with a rolling pin until a fine mixture is formed.

4 Pour all but 1 tbsp oil from the pan and fry the garlic and onion for 1 minute. Add the chilli powder, sugar, a pinch of salt and the water and bring to the boil.

5 Stir in the peanuts. Reduce the heat and simmer for 4–5 minutes until the sauce thickens. Add the lemon juice and leave to cool.

6 Arrange the vegetables in a serving dish and spoon the peanut dressing into the centre. Garnish and serve.

COOK'S TIP

If necessary, you can prepare the peanut dressing in advance and then store it in the refrigerator for up to 12 hours before serving.

Grilled (Broiled) Vegetable Salad with Mustard Dressing

The vegetables for this dish are best prepared well in advance and chilled before serving.

Serves 4

INGREDIENTS

1 courgette (zucchini), sliced
1 yellow (bell) pepper, sliced
1 aubergine (eggplant), sliced
1 fennel bulb, cut into eight
1 red onion, cut into eight
16 cherry tomatoes
3 tbsp olive oil

1 garlic clove, crushed
fresh rosemary sprigs, to garnish

DRESSING:
4 tbsp olive oil
2 tbsp balsamic vinegar
2 tsp chopped rosemary

1 tsp Dijon mustard
1 tsp clear honey
2 tsp lemon juice

1 Put all of the vegetables except for the cherry tomatoes on to a baking tray (cookie sheet).

2 Mix the oil and garlic and brush over the vegetables. Cook under a medium-hot grill (broiler) for 10 minutes until tender and beginning to char. Leave to cool. Spoon the vegetables into a serving bowl.

3 Mix the dressing ingredients and pour over the vegetables. Cover and chill for 1 hour. Garnish and serve.

COOK'S TIP

This dish could also be served warm – heat the dressing in a pan and then toss into the vegetables.

COOK'S TIP

Balsamic vinegar is made in and around Modena in Italy. It is dark and mellow with a sweet-sour flavour. Although it is rather expensive, you only need a small amount to give a wonderful taste to the dressing. If it is unavailable, use sherry vinegar or white wine vinegar instead.

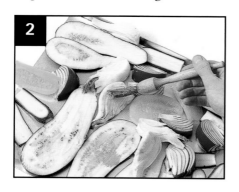

Red Cabbage & Pear Salad

Red cabbage is much underused – it is a colourful and tasty ingredient which is perfect with fruits, such as pears or apples.

Serves 4

INGREDIENTS

350 g/12 oz/4 cups red cabbage,
  finely shredded
2 Conference pears,
  thinly sliced
4 spring onions (scallions), sliced
1 carrot, grated

fresh chives, to garnish
lollo biondo leaves, to serve

DRESSING:
4 tbsp pear juice
1 tsp wholegrain mustard
3 tbsp olive oil
1 tbsp garlic wine vinegar
1 tbsp chopped chives

1 Toss the cabbage, pears and spring onions (scallions) together in a bowl.

2 Line a serving dish with lettuce leaves and spoon the cabbage and pear mixture into the centre.

3 Sprinkle the carrot into the centre of the cabbage to form a domed pile.

4 To make the dressing, mix together the pear juice, wholegrain mustard, olive oil, garlic wine vinegar and chives.

5 Pour the dressing over the salad, garnish and serve immediately.

VARIATION

Experiment with different types of salad leaves. The slightly bitter flavour of chicory (endive) or radicchio would work well with the sweetness of the pears.

COOK'S TIP

Mix the salad just before serving to prevent the colour from the red cabbage bleeding into the other ingredients.

Alfalfa, Beetroot & Spinach Salad

*This is a really refreshing salad that must be assembled just before serving
to prevent all of the ingredients being tainted pink by the beetroot.*

Serves 4

INGREDIENTS

100 g/3¹/₂ oz baby spinach
75 g/2³/₄ oz alfalfa sprouts
2 celery sticks, sliced
4 cooked beetroot, cut into eight

DRESSING:
4 tbsp olive oil
1¹/₂ tbsp garlic wine vinegar
1 garlic clove, crushed

2 tsp clear honey
1 tbsp chopped chives

1 Place the spinach and alfalfa sprouts in a large bowl and mix together.

2 Add the celery and mix well.

3 Toss in the beetroot and mix well.

4 To make the dressing, mix the oil, wine vinegar, garlic, honey and chopped chives.

5 Pour the dressing over the salad, toss well and serve immediately.

VARIATION

*Add the segments of 1 large orange
to the salad to make it even more
colourful and refreshing.
Replace the garlic wine vinegar
with a different flavoured oil such
as chilli or herb, if you prefer.*

COOK'S TIP

*If the spinach leaves are too large,
tear them up rather than cutting
them because cutting bruises
the leaves.*

COOK'S TIP

*Alfalfa sprouts should be available
from most supermarkets, if not,
use bean sprouts instead.*

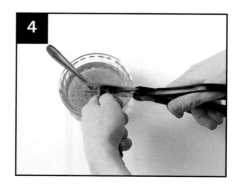

Desserts

Vegetarian or not, confirmed pudding lovers feel a meal is lacking if there isn't a tempting dessert to finish off with. Desserts help to satisfy a deep-seated desire for something sweet and they make us feel good. However, they are often loaded with fat and sugar which are notorious for piling on the calories. Some of the recipes in this chapter offer the perfect solution – they are light, but full of flavour, so you can still enjoy that sweet treat without the bulging waistline!

This chapter contains a wonderful selection of irresistible desserts, perfect for rounding off a meal. There are simple fruit fools that are quick to make, cakes, exotic fruit tarts and all time favourites, such as chocolate cheesecake and steamed sponges. As mentioned in the introduction, vegetarian alternatives may be used for cream and milk in the recipes, and vegetarian gelatine (gelozone) has been used in those recipes that require setting. So take your pick and dip into a delicious dessert!

Raspberry Fool

*This dish is very easy to make and can be made in advance
and stored in the refrigerator.*

Serves 4

INGREDIENTS

300 g/10¹/₂ oz fresh raspberries
50 g/1³/₄ oz/¹/₄ cup icing
(confectioners') sugar

300 ml/¹/₂ pint/1¹/₄ cups crème
fraîche, plus extra to decorate
¹/₂ tsp vanilla essence

2 egg whites
raspberries and lemon balm leaves,
to decorate

1 Put the raspberries and icing
(confectioners') sugar in a
food processor or blender and
blend until smooth.

2 Reserve 1 tablespoon per
portion of crème fraîche for
decorating.

3 Put the vanilla essence and
crème fraîche in a bowl and
stir in the raspberry mixture.

4 Whisk the egg whites in a
separate mixing bowl until
stiff peaks form. Fold the egg
whites into the raspberry mixture

using a metal spoon, until fully
incorporated.

5 Spoon the raspberry fool into
serving dishes and chill for at
least 1 hour. Decorate with the
reserved crème fraîche, raspberries
and lemon balm leaves and serve.

COOK'S TIP

*Although this dessert is best made
with fresh raspberries in season, an
acceptable result can be achieved
with frozen raspberries, which are
available from most supermarkets.*

VARIATION

*This recipe is also
delicious made
with strawberries
or blackberries.*

COOK'S TIP

*Crème fraîche is usually vegetarian,
however, low-fat versions tend to
contain gelatine so remember to
read the label first.*

Chocolate Mousse

This is a light and fluffy, but fruity-tasting mousse which is delicious with a fresh fruit sauce.

Serves 8

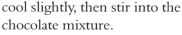

INGREDIENTS

100 g/3^1/$_2$ oz dark chocolate, melted
300 ml/^{1}/$_2$ pint/1^1/$_4$ cups natural (unsweetened) yogurt
150 ml/^{1}/$_4$ pint/^{2}/$_3$ cup quark
4 tbsp caster (superfine) sugar
1 tbsp orange juice

1 tbsp brandy
1^1/$_2$ tsp gelozone
9 tbsp cold water
2 large egg whites

coarsely grated dark and white chocolate and orange zest, to decorate

1 Put the melted chocolate, natural (unsweetened) yogurt, quark, caster (superfine) sugar, orange juice and brandy in a food processor and blend for 30 seconds. Transfer the mixture to a large bowl.

2 Sprinkle the gelozone over the water and stir until dissolved.

3 In a small saucepan, bring the gelozone and water to the boil for 2 minutes. Leave to cool slightly, then stir into the chocolate mixture.

4 Whisk the egg whites until stiff peaks form and fold into the chocolate mixture using a metal spoon.

5 Line a 850 ml/1^1/$_2$ pint loaf tin (pan) with cling film (plastic wrap). Spoon the mousse into the tin (pan). Chill for 2 hours in the refrigerator until set. Turn the mousse out on to a plate, decorate and serve.

COOK'S TIP

For a quick fruit sauce, blend a can of mandarin segments in natural juice in a food processor and press through a sieve. Stir in 1 tbsp clear honey and serve with the mousse.

Berry Cheesecake

Use a mixture of berries, such as blueberries, blackberries, raspberries and strawberries, for a really fruity cheesecake.

Serves 8

INGREDIENTS

BASE:
75 g/2³/4 oz/6 tbsp vegetarian
  margarine
175 g/6 oz oatmeal biscuits
50 g/1³/4 oz/³/4 cup desiccated
  (shredded) coconut

TOPPING:
1¹/2 tsp gelozone
9 tbsp cold water
125 ml/4 fl oz/¹/2 cup evaporated
  milk
1 egg

6 tbsp light brown sugar
450 g/1 lb/2 cups soft cream cheese
350 g/12 oz/1³/4 cups mixed berries
2 tbsp clear honey

1 Put the margarine in a saucepan and heat until melted. Put the biscuits in a food processor and blend until smooth or crush finely with a rolling pin. Stir into the margarine with the coconut.

2 Press the mixture into a base-lined 20 cm/8 inch spring-form tin (pan) and chill whilst preparing the filling.

3 To make the topping, sprinkle the gelozone over the water and stir to dissolve. Bring to the boil and boil for 2 minutes. Let cool slightly.

4 Put the milk, egg, sugar and soft cream cheese in a bowl and beat until smooth. Stir in 50 g/1³/4 oz/¹/4 cup of the berries. Stir in the gelozone in a stream, stirring constantly, until fully incorporated.

5 Spoon the mixture on to the biscuit base and return to the refrigerator for 2 hours or until set.

6 Remove the cheesecake from the tin (pan) and transfer to a serving plate. Arrange the remaining berries on top of the cheesecake and drizzle the honey over the top. Serve.

COOK'S TIP

Warm the honey slightly to make it runnier and easier to drizzle.

Steamed Coffee Sponge & Sauce

This sponge pudding is very light and is delicious with a coffee or chocolate sauce.

Serves 4

INGREDIENTS

2 tbsp vegetarian margarine
2 tbsp soft brown sugar
2 eggs
50 g/1³/4 oz/¹/3 cup plain (all-purpose) flour

³/4 tsp baking powder
6 tbsp milk
1 tsp coffee flavouring (extract)

SAUCE:
300 ml/¹/2 pint/1¹/4 cups milk
1 tbsp soft brown sugar
1 tsp cocoa powder
2 tbsp cornflour (cornstarch)

1 Lightly grease a 600 ml/1 pint heatproof pudding basin. Cream the margarine and sugar until light and fluffy and beat in the eggs.

2 Gradually stir in the flour and baking powder and then the milk and coffee flavouring (extract) to make a smooth batter.

3 Spoon the mixture into the prepared pudding basin and cover with a pleated piece of baking parchment and then a pleated piece of foil, securing around the bowl with string. Place in a steamer or large pan and half fill with boiling water. Cover and steam for 1–1¹/4 hours or until cooked through.

4 To make the sauce, put the milk, soft brown sugar and cocoa powder in a pan and heat until the sugar dissolves. Blend the cornflour (cornstarch) with 4 tablespoons of cold water to make a paste and stir into the pan. Bring to the boil, stirring until thickened. Cook over a gentle heat for 1 minute.

5 Turn the pudding out on to a serving plate and spoon the sauce over the top. Serve.

COOK'S TIP

The pudding is covered with pleated paper and foil to allow it to rise. The foil will react with the steam and must therefore not be placed directly against the pudding.

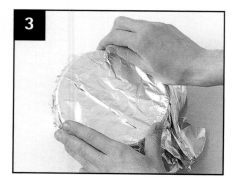

Fruit Brûlée

This is a cheat's brûlée, in that yogurt is used to cover a base of fruit, before being sprinkled with sugar and grilled (broiled).

Serves 4

INGREDIENTS

4 plums, stoned and sliced
2 cooking apples, peeled and sliced
1 tsp ground ginger
600 ml/1 pint/2$^{1}/_{2}$ cups Greek-style yogurt

2 tbsp icing (confectioners') sugar, sieved
1 tsp almond essence

75 g/2$^{3}/_{4}$ oz/$^{1}/_{3}$ cup demerara (brown crystal) sugar

1 Put the plums and apples in a saucepan with 2 tablespoons of water and cook for 7–10 minutes until tender but not mushy. Leave to cool, then stir in the ginger.

2 Using a slotted spoon, spoon the mixture into the base of a shallow serving dish.

3 Mix together the Greek-style yogurt, icing (confectioners') sugar and almond essence and spoon on to the fruit, to cover the fruit completely.

4 Sprinkle the demerara (brown crystal) sugar over the top of the yogurt and cook under a hot grill (broiler) for 3–4 minutes or until the sugar has dissolved and formed a crust. Chill in the refrigerator for 1 hour and serve.

COOK'S TIP

Use any variety of fruit, such as mixed berries or mango pieces, for this dessert, but do not poach them.

VARIATION

You can vary the fruit in this dish, depending on what is in season – try fresh apricots or peaches. Alternatively, use a 400 g/14 oz can of fruit cocktail.

Pear Cake

This is a really moist cake, flavoured with chopped pears and cinnamon.

Serves 12

INGREDIENTS

4 pears, peeled and cored
vegetarian margarine, for greasing
2 tbsp water
200 g/7 oz/1½ cups plain (all-
purpose) flour

2 tsp baking powder
100 g/3½ oz/½ cup soft light
brown sugar
4 tbsp milk

2 tbsp clear honey, plus extra to
drizzle
2 tsp ground cinnamon
2 egg whites

1 Grease and line the base of a 20 cm/8 inch cake tin (pan).

2 Put 1 pear in a food processor with the water and blend until almost smooth. Transfer to a mixing bowl.

3 Sieve in the plain (all-purpose) flour and baking powder. Beat in the sugar, milk, honey and cinnamon and mix well with your fingers.

4 Chop all but one of the remaining pears and add to the mixture.

5 Whisk the egg whites until peaking and gently fold into the mixture until fully blended.

6 Slice the remaining pear and arrange in a fan pattern on the base of the tin (pan).

7 Spoon the cake mixture into the tin (pan) and cook in a preheated oven, 150°C/300°F/Gas Mark 2, for 1¼–1½ hours or until cooked through.

8 Remove the cake from the oven and leave to cool in the tin (pan) for 10 minutes.

9 Turn the cake out on to a wire cooling rack and drizzle with honey. Leave to cool completely, then cut into slices to serve.

COOK'S TIP

To test if the cake is cooked through, insert a skewer into the centre – if it comes out clean the cake is cooked. If not, return the cake to the oven and test at frequent intervals.

Fruit & Nut Loaf

*This loaf is like a fruit bread which may be served warm or cold,
perhaps spread with a little vegetarian margarine or butter or topped with jam.*

Makes 1 loaf

INGREDIENTS

225 g/8 oz/1^3/4 cups white
   bread flour, plus extra for dusting

^{1}/2 tsp salt

1 tbsp vegetarian margarine, plus
   extra for greasing

2 tbsp soft light brown sugar

100 g/3^1/2 oz/^{2}/3 cup sultanas
   (golden raisins)

50 g/1^3/4 oz/^{1}/2 cup no-need to soak
   dried apricots, chopped

50 g/1^3/4 oz/^{1}/2 cup chopped
   hazelnuts

2 tsp easy-blend dried yeast

6 tbsp orange juice

6 tbsp natural (unsweetened) yogurt

2 tbsp sieved apricot jam

1 Sieve the flour and salt into a mixing bowl. Rub in the margarine and stir in the sugar, sultanas (golden raisins), apricots, nuts and yeast.

2 Warm the orange juice in a saucepan but do not allow to boil.

3 Stir the warm orange juice into the flour mixture with the natural (unsweetened) yogurt and bring the mixture together to form a dough.

4 Knead the dough on a lightly floured surface for 5 minutes until smooth and elastic. Shape into a round and place on a lightly greased baking tray (cookie sheet). Cover with a clean tea towel (dish cloth) and leave to rise in a warm place until doubled in size.

5 Cook the loaf in a preheated oven, 220°C/425°F/Gas Mark 7, for 35–40 minutes until cooked through. Transfer to a cooling rack and brush with the apricot jam. Leave to cool before serving.

COOK'S TIP

To test if the loaf is cooked through – tap the base and if it sounds hollow, it's cooked.

VARIATION

You can vary the nuts according to whatever you have at hand – try chopped walnuts or almonds.

Desserts

Mixed Fruit Crumble

*I have used tropical fruits in this crumble, flavoured with ginger
and coconut, for something a little different and very tasty.*

Serves 4

INGREDIENTS

2 mangoes, sliced
1 paw paw, seeded and sliced
225 g/8 oz fresh pineapple, cubed
1½ tsp ground ginger
100 g/3½ oz/8 tbsp vegetarian
 margarine

100 g/3½ oz/½ cup soft light
 brown sugar
175 g/6 oz/1½ cups plain (all-
 purpose) flour

50 g/1¾ oz desiccated (shredded)
 coconut, plus extra to decorate

1 Place the fruit in a pan
with ½ tsp of the ginger,
25 g/1 oz/2 tbsp of the margarine
and 50 g/1¾ oz/¼ cup of the
sugar. Cook over a gentle heat for
10 minutes until the fruit softens.
Spoon the fruit into the base of a
shallow ovenproof dish.

2 Mix the flour and remaining
ginger together. Rub in the
remaining margarine until the
mixture resembles fine
breadcrumbs. Stir in the
remaining sugar and the coconut

and spoon over the fruit to
cover completely.

3 Cook the crumble in a
preheated oven at 180°C/
350°F/Gas Mark 4 for about
40 minutes or until the top is crisp.
Decorate and serve.

VARIATION

*Paw-paws (papayas) have an
orangey yellow skin and should
yield to gentle pressure.*

VARIATION

*Use other fruits, such as
plums, apples or
blackberries, as a
fruit base and add
chopped nuts to the topping
instead of the coconut.*

240

Autumn Fruit Bread Pudding

*This is like a summer pudding, but it uses fruits which appear later in the year,
such as apples, pears and blackberries, as a succulent filling.*

Serves 8

INGREDIENTS

900 g/2 lb/4 cups mixed blackberries,
  chopped apples, chopped pears
150 g/5¹/₂ oz/³/₄ cup soft light
  brown sugar

1 tsp cinnamon
225 g/8 oz white bread,
  thinly sliced, crusts removed

1 Place the fruit in a large saucepan with the soft light brown sugar, cinnamon and 100 ml/3¹/₂ fl oz of water, stir and bring to the boil. Reduce the heat and simmer for 5–10 minutes so that the fruits soften but still hold their shape.

2 Meanwhile, line the base and sides of a 850 ml/1¹/₂ pint pudding basin with the bread slices, ensuring that there are no gaps between the pieces of bread.

3 Spoon the fruit into the centre of the bread-lined bowl and cover the fruit with the remaining bread.

4 Place a saucer on top of the bread and weight it down. Chill in the refrigerator overnight.

5 Turn the pudding out on to a serving plate and serve immediately.

COOK'S TIP

Stand the pudding on a plate when chilling to catch any juices that run down the sides of the basin.

COOK'S TIP

This pudding would be delicious served with vegetarian vanilla ice cream to counteract the tartness of the blackberries.

Apple Fritters & Almond Sauce

These apple fritters are coated in a light, spiced batter
and deep-fried until crisp and golden. Serve warm.

Serves 4

INGREDIENTS

100 g/3^1/$_2$ oz/^{3}/$_4$ cup plain (all-
    purpose) flour
pinch of salt
^{1}/$_2$ tsp ground cinnamon
12 tbsp warm water
4 tsp vegetable oil

2 egg whites
2 dessert (eating) apples, peeled
vegetable or sunflower oil, for deep-
    frying
caster (superfine) sugar and
    cinnamon, to decorate

SAUCE:
150 ml/^{1}/$_4$ pint/1^1/$_4$ cups natural
    (unsweetened) yogurt
^{1}/$_2$ tsp almond essence
2 tsp clear honey

1 Sieve the flour and salt into a mixing bowl.

2 Add the cinnamon and mix well. Stir in the water and oil to make a smooth batter.

3 Whisk the egg whites until stiff peaks form and fold into the batter.

4 Using a sharp knife, cut the apples into chunks and dip the pieces of apple into the batter to coat.

5 Heat the oil for deep-frying to 180°C/350°F or until a cube of bread browns in 30 seconds. Fry the apple pieces, in batches, for 3–4 minutes until golden brown and puffy.

6 Remove the apple fritters from the oil with a slotted spoon and leave to drain on absorbent paper towels.

7 Mix the caster (superfine) sugar and cinnamon and sprinkle over the fritters.

8 Mix the sauce ingredients in a serving bowl and serve with the fritters.

VARIATION

Use pieces of banana or pineapple instead of the apple, if you prefer.

Cherry Pancakes

This dish can be made with either fresh pitted cherries or canned cherries for speed.

Serves 4

INGREDIENTS

FILLING:
400 g/14 oz can pitted cherries, plus juice
$^1/_2$ tsp almond essence
$^1/_2$ tsp mixed spice
2 tbsp cornflour (cornstarch)

PANCAKES:
100 g/3$^1/_2$ oz/$^3/_4$ cup plain (all-purpose) flour
pinch of salt
2 tbsp chopped mint
1 egg

300 ml/$^1/_2$ pint/1$^1/_4$ cups milk
vegetable oil, for frying
icing (confectioners' sugar) and toasted flaked (slivered) almonds, to decorate

1 Put the cherries and 300 ml/½ pint/1¼ cups of the juice in a pan with the almond essence and mixed spice. Stir in the cornflour (cornstarch) and bring to the boil, stirring until thickened and clear. Set aside until required.

2 To make the pancakes, sieve the flour into a bowl with the salt. Add the chopped mint and make a well in the centre. Gradually beat in the egg and milk to make a smooth batter.

3 Heat 1 tbsp of oil in an 18 cm/ 7 inch frying pan (skillet); pour off the oil when hot. Add just enough batter to coat the base of the frying pan (skillet) and cook for 1–2 minutes or until the underside is cooked. Flip the pancake over and cook for 1 minute. Remove from the pan and keep warm. Heat 1 tbsp of the oil in the pan again and repeat to use up all the batter.

4 Spoon a quarter of the cherry filling on to a quarter of each pancake and fold the pancake into a cone shape. Dust with icing (confectioners') sugar and sprinkle the flaked (slivered) almonds over the top. Serve.

VARIATION

Use other fillings, such as gooseberries or blackberries, as an alternative to the cherries.

Lemon & Lime Syllabub

This dessert is rich but absolutely delicious. It is not, however, for the calorie conscious as it contains a high proportion of cream, but it's well worth blowing the diet for!

Serves 4

INGREDIENTS

50 g/1³/₄ oz/¹/₄ cup caster
  (superfine) sugar
grated zest and juice of
  1 small lemon
grated zest and juice of
  1 small lime

50 ml/2 fl oz/4 tbsp Marsala
  or medium sherry
300 ml/¹/₂ pint/1¹/₄ cups double
  (heavy) cream
lime and lemon zest, to decorate

1 Put the sugar, fruit juices and zest and sherry in a bowl, mix well and leave to infuse for 2 hours.

2 Add the cream to the mixture and whisk until it just holds its shape.

3 Spoon the mixture into 4 tall serving glasses and chill in the refrigerator for 2 hours.

4 Decorate with lime and lemon zest and serve.

COOK'S TIP

Serve with almond biscuits or uncoated florentines. Do not overwhip the cream when adding to the lemon and lime mixture as it may curdle.

VARIATION

For an alternative citrus flavour substitute two oranges for the lemon and lime, if you prefer.

COOK'S TIP

Replace the double (heavy) cream with natural (unsweetened) yogurt for a healthier version of this dessert, or use half quantities of both. Whisk the cream before adding to the yogurt.

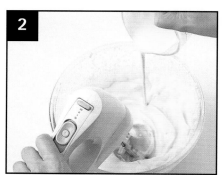

Banana & Mango Tart

*Bananas and mangoes are a great combination of colours and flavours,
especially when topped with toasted coconut chips.*

Serves 8

INGREDIENTS

PASTRY:
20 cm/8 inch baked pastry case

FILLING:
2 small ripe bananas
1 mango, sliced
$3^1/2$ tbsp cornflour (cornstarch)
50 g/$1^3/4$ oz/6 tbsp demerara (brown crystal) sugar

300 ml/$^1/2$ pint/$1^1/4$ cups soya milk
150 ml/$^1/4$ pint/$^2/3$ cup coconut milk
1 tsp vanilla essence
toasted coconut chips, to decorate

1 Slice the bananas and arrange half in the baked pastry case with half of the mango pieces.

2 Put the cornflour (cornstarch) and sugar in a saucepan and mix together. Slowly stir in the soya and coconut milks until combined and cook over a low heat, beating until the mixture thickens.

3 Stir in the vanilla essence then pour the mixture over the fruit.

4 Top with the remaining fruit and toasted coconut chips. Chill in the refrigerator for 1 hour before serving.

COOK'S TIP

Coconut chips are available in some supermarkets and most health food shops. It is worth using them as they look much more attractive and are not as sweet as desiccated (shredded) coconut.

COOK'S TIP

Choose mangoes with shiny and unblemished skins. To test whether they are ripe, gently cup the mango in your hand and squeeze gently – the mango should yield slightly to the touch.

Chocolate & Tofu (Bean Curd) Cheesecake

This cheesecake takes a little time to prepare and cook but is well worth the effort.
It is quite rich and is good served or decorated with a little fresh fruit, such as sliced strawberries.

Serves 12

INGREDIENTS

100 g/3$\frac{1}{2}$ oz/$\frac{3}{4}$ cup plain (all-purpose) flour

100 g/3$\frac{1}{2}$ oz/$\frac{3}{4}$ cup ground almonds

200 g/7 oz/$\frac{3}{4}$ cup demerara (brown crystal) sugar

150 g/5$\frac{1}{2}$ oz/10 tbsp vegetarian margarine

675 g/1$\frac{1}{2}$ lb firm tofu (bean curd)

175 ml/6 fl oz/$\frac{3}{4}$ cup vegetable oil

125 ml/4 fl oz/$\frac{1}{2}$ cup orange juice

175 ml/6 fl oz/$\frac{3}{4}$ cup brandy

50 g/1$\frac{3}{4}$ oz/6 tbsp cocoa powder, plus extra to decorate

2 tsp almond essence

icing (confectioners') sugar and Cape gooseberries, to decorate

1 Put the flour, ground almonds and 1 tablespoon of the sugar in a bowl and mix well. Rub the margarine into the mixture to form a dough.

2 Lightly grease and line the base of a 23 cm/9 inch spring-form tin (pan). Press the dough into the base of the tin (pan) to cover, pushing the dough right up to the edge of the tin (pan).

3 Roughly chop the tofu (bean curd) and put in a food processor with all of the remaining ingredients and blend until smooth and creamy. Pour over the base in the tin (pan) and cook in a preheated oven, 160°C/325°F/Gas Mark 3, for 1–1$\frac{1}{4}$ hours or until set.

4 Leave to cool in the tin (pan) for 5 minutes, then remove from the tin (pan) and chill in the refrigerator. Dust with icing (confectioners') sugar and cocoa powder. Decorate and serve.

COOK'S TIP

Cape gooseberries make an attractive decoration for many desserts. Peel open the papery husks to expose the bright orange fruits.

Chocolate Fudge Pudding

*This pudding has a hidden surprise when cooked as it separates
to give a rich chocolate sauce at the bottom of the dish.*

Serves 4

INGREDIENTS

50 g/1³/₄ oz/4 tbsp vegetarian
  margarine, plus extra for greasing
75 g/2³/₄ oz/6 tbsp soft light brown
  sugar
2 eggs, beaten
350 ml/12 fl oz/1¹/₄ cups milk

50 g/1³/₄ oz chopped walnuts
40 g/1¹/₂ oz/¹/₄ cup plain (all-
  purpose) flour
2 tbsp cocoa powder

icing (confectioners') sugar and
  cocoa, to dust

1 Lightly grease a 1 litre/
1³/₄ pint ovenproof dish.

2 Cream together the
margarine and sugar in a
large mixing bowl until fluffy.
Beat in the eggs.

3 Gradually stir in the milk and
add the walnuts.

4 Sieve the flour and cocoa
powder into the mixture and
fold in gently, with a metal spoon,
until well mixed.

5 Spoon the mixture into the
dish and cook in a preheated
oven at 180°C/350°F/Gas Mark 4
for 35–40 minutes or until the
sponge is cooked.

6 Dust with icing
(confectioners') sugar and
cocoa powder and serve.

COOK'S TIP

*Serve this pudding with crème
fraîche for a luxuriously rich dessert.*

VARIATION

*Add 1–2 tbsp brandy or rum to the
mixture for a slightly alcoholic
pudding, or 1–2 tbsp orange juice
for a child-friendly version.*

Index

Index compiled by Lydia Darbyshire

Catherine

DUCHESS OF CAMBRIDGE

ANNIE BULLEN

Catherine Middleton is the young woman who waited patiently for her prince and won the heart of a nation. The Duchess of Cambridge, and the future Queen Consort, still known popularly as 'Kate', comes not from the ranks of royalty or the aristocracy, but from the middle classes. Her parents became prosperous through hard work and they used their wealth to give their daughter an exceptional education, as well as a happy and stable home life.

Clever and sporty Catherine Middleton, educated at prestigious Marlborough College, met Prince William, second in line to the British throne, at St Andrews University in Scotland. Their love story has stood the test of time and seen them pronounced man and wife in historic Westminster Abbey, witnessed by a worldwide audience, in April 2011.

Catherine's own story is one of patience, devotion and loyalty. She is a woman of great inner strength and serenity, with a vivacious, natural charm, whose love for Prince William, through years of friendship and romance, never wavered. She is calm, confident, sensible and kind, smiling and self-assured, even under pressure from the media and the demanding role that will, from now on, be hers for life.

DATES & EVENTS

1982 Catherine (Kate) Middleton is born on 9 January 1982 at the Royal Berkshire Hospital, Reading.

1984 Catherine and her family move to Amman, Jordan for two years.

1987 Catherine attends St Andrew's Preparatory School, in Pangbourne, Berkshire.

1995 Catherine boards at Downe House near Newbury for two terms, but leaves to go to Marlborough College, in Wiltshire.

2000–01 Catherine enjoys a 'gap year', studying art and Italian in Florence, crewing and sailing in the Solent, and undertaking an Operation Raleigh challenge in Chile, Latin America.

2001 She goes up to St Andrews University to study Art History; she meets fellow student 'William Wales'.

2002 Catherine and Prince William, with two other friends, move into a student house in Hope Street, St Andrews.

2003 Catherine attends Prince William's 21st birthday party at Windsor Castle in June; in September, she shares a house with William during their third year at university.

2004 The couple are pictured together while on a skiing holiday at Klosters, Switzerland.

2005 Catherine and William graduate from St Andrews; they each achieve an upper second-class (2:1) degree. The couple fly to Kenya for a holiday.

2006 The couple join friends on a skiing holiday at Klosters in January. Catherine is invited to the wedding of Laura Parker Bowles, Prince William's step-sister. In November, she starts work as a buyer with fashion chain Jigsaw.

2006 In December, Catherine watches as Prince William passes out of Sandhurst, receiving his commission as a second lieutenant in the Household Cavalry.

2007 In March, Prince William starts training with his regiment at Bovington Camp, in Dorset. In April, he tells Catherine that their relationship is at an end – but by June the couple are reconciled. In October, Catherine is invited to Balmoral, the Royal Family's home in Scotland, for the weekend.

2008 In April, Catherine is at William's side as he graduates from the RAF at Cranwell; in June, she watches as he is invested as a Knight of the Garter. They enjoy a holiday together at Birkhall, on the Balmoral estate.

2009 In May, the couple are photographed together at a polo match.

2010 In January, Catherine applauds as William graduates from an advanced helicopter flying course, receiving his wings from his father, the Prince of Wales. In March, William and Catherine join her parents on holiday in Courchevel, France.

2010 On 16 November Clarence House announces William and Catherine's engagement.

2011 In February, Catherine attends her first public engagement with William when they name a lifeboat in Anglesey. They later visit St Andrews, their old university, together. In March, William and Catherine make an official visit to Northern Ireland.

2011 On 29 April Catherine Middleton is married to Prince William at Westminster Abbey. The couple receive the titles Duke and Duchess of Cambridge, from Her Majesty The Queen.

2011 In July, the Duke and Duchess of Cambridge make official visits to Canada and the United States. In October, Catherine carries out her first solo engagement, a charity dinner at Clarence House.

Catherine MIDDLETON

Catherine Elizabeth Middleton, the first-born of the family, arrived on a cold Saturday, 9 January 1982, at the Royal Berkshire Hospital in Reading, not far from her parents' home in the ancient village of Bradfield Southend, in Berkshire. Her mother Carole and father, Michael, were married in June 1980, moving into the red-brick house that they had spent eight months renovating and repairing.

The dark-haired infant was christened at the local church and less than two years later, in September 1983, her sister Pippa (Philippa Charlotte) was born.

Not long afterwards the family moved to Amman in Jordan where Catherine's father, a British Airways manager, was posted. Toddler Catherine learnt to speak Arabic at the Al-Saheera nursery school, which she attended until the Middletons returned to Berkshire in 1986. The family was completed in April 1987 when a brother, James, was born.

The three children, nurtured by a close and loving family, plenty of friends and a comfortable country life, enjoyed their childhood, taking long walks together, and playing dressing-up games and musical statues. They enjoyed family meals and, as the children grew, their friends were welcomed by Carole, who would cook treats for them, including imaginative cakes.

Above: Catherine Middleton, aged three, enjoys a family holiday in the Lake District.

Above: Catherine (left) in Jerash, Jordan with her father, Michael and younger sister, Pippa.

Right: Catherine smiles from the Royal Box at Cheltenham Racecourse, in March 2007.

CATHERINE'S *Family*

By the time Catherine was born, in 1982, the Middleton family were able to afford the best in life for their children. But it had not always been so, especially for her mother's family. Carole Goldsmith's ancestors, the Harrisons, were miners, working in the coal pits of Durham, in north-east England, and with others in the mines, were prey to poverty and diseases caused by the hard and dangerous work. Carole's great-grandfather, Thomas Harrison, escaped the mines and learnt the carpenter's trade, moving from the north to Southall, in London. In 1953 his 18-year-old daughter, Dorothy, an ambitious young woman, married Ronald Goldsmith, a lorry driver, general handyman and sometime baker.

Her daughter Carole, Catherine's mother, was born in 1955, living for the first 11 years of her life in a modest apartment but moving, in 1966, to a brand new semi-detached house in Norwood Green, West London. Carole was determined and ambitious, like her mother, and passed the stringent tests to become a BOAC (now British Airways) air

Catherine's paternal grandfather, Peter Middleton, a fighter-pilot during the Second World War, later became an airline captain, flying Prince Philip, Duke of Edinburgh in a Britannia, on a royal tour of South America in 1962. Mr Middleton, who retired to the Hampshire village of Vernham Dean, died aged 90, just days before the official announcement of his granddaughter's engagement to Prince William in November 2010.

Above right: Sisters Pippa (left) and Catherine Middleton step out together in June 2008.

Right: Carole and Michael Middleton, Catherine's parents, pose for photographers at their Berkshire home.

Above: Catherine Middleton and her mother, Carole, enjoy a Christmas shopping trip in London, in 2005.

stewardess in the 1970s. It was while working for the airline that she met Michael Middleton, a well-to-do and well-connected manager there. His Leeds-based ancestors were successful lawyers and mill owners.

Carole and Michael's was a lengthy courtship before they settled down to married life and, eventually, new careers as entrepreneurial business people. Michael continued to work for British Airways while Carole, now with three young children to look after, became fully involved in village life, taking the children to playgroup and nursery school – and to children's parties. She soon discovered the idea of making up and selling children's party bags, a must for successful occasions, but time-consuming for working mothers to organize. The business took off, and had to move out of the family home into rented premises nearby. In time the company grew to become a successful online business, supplying everything needed for all types of parties. Michael Middleton gave up his British Airways job to join the family business and, in 1995, the couple were able to afford a substantial house in the nearby village of Bucklebury and to send their children to private schools.

A HAPPY *Childhood*

Although Catherine had attended the English-speaking Al-Saheera nursery school during the family's brief stay in Jordan, her earliest classroom memories are of the co-educational St Andrew's Preparatory School in Pangbourne, a few miles from her home. The school, based in a large Victorian building and set in attractive woodland, taught the fee-paying pupils in small groups of between 15 to 20.

The naturally sporty Catherine was in her element. Wearing her green blazer, white shirt and kilt, she studied hard and played hard – breaking the school high-jump record, becoming a member of the school swimming team and an outstanding netball, rounders and tennis player. In her last year at St Andrew's she was named the best all-round sportswoman. She enjoyed her days there so much that, at the age of 11, she became a weekly boarder, living in from Sunday night until Friday evening. At this stage in her life, the tall and growing youngster was no great beauty. Her naturally slim form made even skinnier by all the sport she played, she often seemed pale and heavy-eyed, and in her last year at school she wore a brace on her teeth.

Friends remember that she was determined to do as well academically as on the sports field, studying long hours and that this somehow set her apart. Her natural reticence made her seem quiet and shy, especially alongside her younger sister, fellow pupil, Pippa, who was more boisterous and gregarious. Catherine was the one who was often praised for good behaviour. She did not, however, shun the limelight when it came to acting, taking part in several school productions, and it was discovered she had a natural talent for the stage. Many former pupils remember, with a sense of prescience, her starring role in the Victorian melodrama *Murder in the Red Barn*. In one scene, she encounters a fortune-teller, who assures her: 'Soon you will meet a handsome man, a rich gentleman.' 'Will he fall in love with me?' asks Catherine's character. 'And marry me?' 'Indeed he will,' responds the soothsayer. The scene ends with her suitor, William, proposing on bended knee. 'It's all I ever longed for,' cries Catherine. 'Yes, oh yes, dear William!'

Above: Catherine (centre) at St Andrew's School, Pangbourne, Berkshire.

Catherine's good behaviour and quiet self-possession were rewarded in her last year at St Andrew's when she was made a prefect. This had the advantage of the use of the senior common room with its comfortable chairs and a television, a privilege afforded to only a few students.

Left and below: Then and now, Catherine, a cheerful five-year-old and smiling happily on the day her engagement to Prince William is announced.

Prince William would not have been aware of the shy, slender schoolgirl who avidly watched his every move when he visited St Andrew's prep school to compete in hockey, rugby and football matches. St Andrew's was co-educational and boys from Ludgrove, the exclusively male school where both Prince William and Prince Harry boarded, came over to compete in matches. The two schools were only 14 miles (22 km) apart and the Princes, both excelling at sport, were members of their school's sports teams. All the St Andrew's girls, knowing that William would be competing on their playing fields, turned up to watch the matches and to catch a glimpse of the handsome young Prince, and Catherine was no exception.

Back at home, at weekends and during the school holidays, it was unlikely that the young Middleton siblings were ever bored or lacked things to do. Their parents Carole and Michael ensured that there was always plenty going on, while both sets of grandparents were on hand to look after the children, if the family business claimed their parents' attention.

Right: Catherine (centre) pictured at St Andrew's School.

Below: Catherine (centre, front row) an excellent sportswoman, enjoyed playing rounders.

SCHOOLDAYS & HOLIDAYS

Above: Catherine (centre, back row) played in goal defence in the school netball team.

When Catherine reached the age of 13, she had sat and easily passed her Common Entrance exam and was ready to go to secondary school. Her parents' first choice was the exclusive Downe House, a single-sex boarding school near Newbury, in Berkshire, regarded as one of the top educational establishments in Britain. But Catherine struggled to fit in and after two terms she left, heading for the equally exclusive Marlborough College, just outside the town of the same name in the Wiltshire countryside.

Long country walks, meals, and games as a family and with friends, trips to the cinema and exciting holidays were normal activities, while there were visits from Carole's parents, Dorothy and Ronald, who had moved to just a few miles away. Dorothy, an expert needlewoman, taught both girls sewing and embroidery. The children also enjoyed visits to their paternal grandparents, in the pretty Hampshire village of Vernham Dean. It was here that their grandfather Peter, an experienced sailor, built a pirate ship in his large garden so that the children could act out their own adventures. At other times, he would take them down to the Hamble estuary, on the Hampshire coast, and teach them how to sail.

CATHERINE'S *Teens*

Catherine's parents paid £29,000 a year for their elder daughter's education at Marlborough College in Wiltshire, which was founded in 1843 by the Church, for the sons of impoverished clergy. The co-educational school, built around a pretty Queen Anne house on rolling downland, was much more to the new girl's taste. She soon settled down, finding friends, although she still maintained a self-possession which made her stand out from the crowd.

Catherine blossomed at the Wiltshire school and it was here, when she had turned 16, that her true physical beauty became apparent. The pale, shy teenager was transformed into a long-haired, willowy beauty with rosy cheeks and a sense of style. Catherine quickly gained confidence, whilst still hard-working, athletic and easy-going. She has been described by former classmates as popular, level-headed and talented. It was at Marlborough College that she met children of the rich and famous, and enjoyed their company.

Catherine's good judgement and sense of reserve, which became apparent at school, strengthened rather than diminished her popularity. Unlike some of her more rebellious classmates Catherine followed her own moral code, remaining discreet and dignified. She was polite, well-behaved and always kind, without being 'goody-goody'. Fellow pupils recall that, while she enjoyed having fun, she did not join in when 'dorm-parties', with smuggled-in food and drink, were held. Instead she would keep watch for the others, just in case a matron or teacher should be around.

Catherine enjoyed school immensely, and found the freedom to discover herself and not be concerned about what others may think. The girls were not expected to be brilliant, but they had to join in. Many of her fellow pupils were unconventional but most were passionate about something, whether it was writing, painting, history, or music. Catherine became head of her house, Elmhurst, where she is remembered as being very good at helping out, playing games – she was captain of the school hockey team and played in the first pair at tennis – and acting. She won A and B grades for her three A-levels. She was also known for her dependability and loyalty – the qualities she will need to employ for the rest of her life.

Left: Catherine (centre, back row) was an enthusiastic captain of the hockey team at Marlborough College.

ENYOING A
Gap Year

Catherine's A-level examination results in 2000 were good enough to win her a place at most universities. She wanted to pursue an Art History course and some time before, had set her heart on studying for her degree at the Scottish university of St Andrews. As soon as her place was secured, and before she enlisted for another three years of hard work, she was determined to enjoy a year off, partly in preparation for what was to come and partly to pursue traditional gap-year activities.

She started, in September 2000, with a three-month sojourn in the beautiful Italian city of Florence, the city of Michelangelo and Leonardo, where art treasures are on view in every square and every street, and where she could immerse herself in enjoying the Renaissance paintings and sculpture that she would be studying at university. Catherine enrolled in an art and language course at the British Institute. She shared an apartment in the city centre with four girlfriends above a traditional *alimentari,* a grocery. When she was not enjoying the art and architecture and learning to speak Italian, she explored the cobbled streets on foot, taking hundreds of photographs. Photography is one of her passions and Florence was an ideal subject.

When Catherine finally met William, at St Andrews University, they soon discovered they had a gap year experience in common – each had worked in Chile on a programme organized by the Raleigh International Challenge. In fact, the pair had missed each other by just one month. William finished his visit to Chile in December 2000, while Catherine travelled out just after her 19th birthday on 9 January, the following year. She spent the first three weeks trekking through the wilderness with her fellow volunteers before joining in a marine survey, working with British and Chilean scientists. Then came a tough assignment at the village of La Tapera, where the group worked in the blazing sun, chopping, sawing and hammering wood as they helped to build a fire station. Catherine's contribution to the building was working on fitting the windows and cladding the roof.

Left: Catherine, girl about town, in smart-casual jeans and jacket.

The other freshers, including Catherine, arrived at St Andrews – an ancient university in a small town of the same name, 80 miles (128 km) north of Edinburgh – before Prince William, and most of the students were waiting to greet him when he arrived, wearing shirt and jeans and a warm fleece. Both Catherine and William were billeted in the same hall of residence, St Salvator's – known as 'Sally's' – and both were taking the Art History course, which was taught in a grey stone townhouse on North Street. St Salvator's Hall, overlooking the famous golf course and ancient castle, is one of 11 halls of residence, and split into male and female living quarters.

William, like every other male occupant of the hall, soon noticed the quiet and shy brunette who had been voted the prettiest girl there by the end of freshers' week. William and Catherine's story, however, is of a slow-burning romance, an attraction that turned to friendship, companionship and reliance before strengthening into love. Catherine, who liked to go for a run before breakfast, would often arrive in the dining hall, with its impressive stained-glass windows and portraits of philosophers from the Scottish Enlightenment, just before the meal was over. She, like William, chose to eat cereals and fruit, and soon they talked to each other, discovering they had plenty of interests in common.

William remembers those days: 'We were friends for over a year first and it just sort of blossomed. We just spent more time with each other, had a good giggle, lots of fun, and realised we shared the same interests and had a really good time,' he said. Catherine's memories of their first meeting are more personal: 'I actually think I went bright red and sort of scuttled off, feeling very shy.'

The story of the sheer black dress is now history but it was a special moment for the Prince. William, who had paid £200 for a front-row seat for the annual charity fashion show at a St Andrew's hotel, in their second term at university, was bowled over when Catherine, now a friend, sashayed down the catwalk in a revealing dress.

Left: Catherine out shopping, wearing one of her favourite hats.

Right: Stylish in a cowboy hat, Catherine attends the Gatcombe Park Festival.

Although the attraction was mutual, Catherine, loyal to her then boyfriend, wisely kept matters low key, and let love develop slowly. By the time William and Catherine went up for their second year, they had become part of a group of four friends sharing a flat at Hope Street in the town, yet still they managed to keep things discreet, never touching or holding hands in public, arriving at parties separately and, to the world and the sharp-eyed press, they were just good friends.

Catherine
& WILLIAM

William, the handsome young man who will one day be King, could have had his choice of European princesses and aristocratic young women for his bride. But his heart had been captured by an ordinary, although extraordinarily attractive, girl from the Home Counties. Catherine is sporty and shares his love of the outdoor life – a must for anyone joining the Royal Family; she is also cheerful, resourceful and creative.

By the time William's 21st birthday was celebrated with a party at Windsor Castle, in June 2003, it is likely that William and Catherine were romantically linked, although the Prince denied then that he had a steady girlfriend. They were close enough during their third and final years at university to share a secluded cottage on a private estate just outside the town, establishing a cosy domesticity, but still managing to keep the relationship a secret. Their close circle of friends helped, never breaking the code of silence that bound them to the young couple.

It was in April 2004, when Catherine joined William and a group of friends on a skiing holiday at Klosters, Switzerland and they were photographed together, that the press started putting two and two together. There was more speculation later that year when they spent time together on holiday, on an island in the Indian Ocean.

When they graduated, in June 2005, Catherine felt uncertain about the future as William was whisked away on royal duties, starting with a tour to New Zealand, where he represented The Queen. He then began to plan his officer training at Sandhurst, which was due to start in early 2006. Suddenly Catherine, who had just moved into a flat in central London with an old friend from her boarding-school days, found the full glare of the media spotlight on her private life. She coped admirably, accepting the fact that she would have to dress carefully, wear make-up and be suitably coiffured every time she stepped outside in order to face the photographers lying in wait.

Although Prince William continued to deny that marriage was in the air, their relationship was widely accepted, especially after he was photographed kissing Catherine on holiday at Klosters. It seemed, too, that the Royal Family had welcomed her as William's girlfriend when images of William and his father, happy and at ease in her company, were published in newspapers and shown on television.

Left: Catherine joins the royal party skiing at Klosters, Switzerland.

Top left: A training session on the River Thames for a fund-raising rowing event, in June 2007.

Top right: Catherine wears a traditional gown on her graduation day, 23 June 2005, at St Andrews University.

Left: Prince William and Catherine share a private moment at Eton College, where William was taking part in the Old Boys' Field Game, in March 2006.

Above: William and Catherine cheer the England team during the Six Nations rugby match against Italy, at Twickenham in early 2007.

LOVE &
Romance

Catherine and William were young when they met and their path towards true love had its inevitable ups and downs. The year 2006 was busy. William was undergoing army training at Sandhurst where Catherine and her parents watched him graduate in December, shortly after Catherine had started work as an accessories buyer for a fashion chain. Earlier, they had been together at the wedding of William's step-sister, Laura Parker Bowles. But the pressures were showing.

On 14 April 2007 reports of a break in their relationship appeared in newspapers. Prince William was spotted partying, without Catherine. Friends and family knew that he had ended the relationship in the face of mounting media pressure and the tough training regime he was undergoing. Catherine showed fortitude. Inwardly devastated but outwardly, supported by her family, she rallied and carried on, attending parties and high-profile events, where she was invariably surrounded by eligible young men.

By late May, the couple were secretly back together and in June were spotted kissing at William's army camp in Dorset. On 1 July Catherine was a guest at the Concert for Diana, organized by William and his brother, Prince Harry, at Wembley Stadium. The break had shown William and Catherine that they needed the love and companionship each gave the other.

Catherine was increasingly present at public occasions with William, and was invited to join the Royal Family on private visits. She was a guest at William's RAF 'wings' presentation ceremony in April 2008, and she first met her future grandmother-in-law, The Queen at the wedding of Peter Phillips, The Queen's

Above: Prince Harry and Prince William (bottom left) enjoy the music at Wembley in a concert they organized in memory of their late mother, Princess Diana. Catherine (top right) chats to a friend.

Above: Catherine and William together at Cranwell in April 2008 where, earlier, she watched as the Prince received his RAF 'wings' in a graduation ceremony.

Above: Smiling happily, Catherine and William tell the world's press they are to be married. Catherine wears the sapphire ring that was owned by Diana.

grandson, in the same year. In June, she was invited to St George's Chapel, Windsor, to watch William's investiture into the Order of the Garter.

Although, at this time, William and Catherine attended many of their friends' weddings, there was no sign of their own impending nuptials. So the engagement announcement, from Clarence House, on Tuesday 16 November 2010, was a complete surprise and its joyful impact was felt nationwide. Catherine Middleton, wearing the sapphire ring that had once belonged to the Prince's mother Diana, Princess of Wales, took Prince William's arm as they walked into the red and gold grandeur of the Entrée Room at St James's Palace, to face the world's media. Love shone through as the joyful couple, standing closely together, told of their happiness and their plans for the future.

Catherine had no idea that the trip to Kenya in October 2010 was anything more than an exciting holiday. But hidden away in William's rucksack was his late mother's sapphire and diamond ring, which he planned to put on Catherine's finger if she agreed to become his wife. William drove her to the shores of Rutundu Lake, on Mount Kenya where, in a romantic wooden lodge, he proposed. Neither would reveal details but Catherine said: 'It was very romantic and it was very personal.'

A ROYAL
Bride

Radiant and beautiful, Catherine Middleton, clasping her father's hand, stood for a few seconds in the light-filled space inside the West Door of Westminster Abbey. A crimson carpet stretched ahead, marking the length of the nave and the quire to the sanctuary, where her bridegroom, Prince William, wearing his scarlet uniform of Colonel of the Irish Guards, waited for her. Outside the magnificent, historic Abbey, a million well-wishers filled the parks and streets, happy to be part of the royal love story.

Catherine's transformation from commoner to Duchess, from single woman to wife, began as she started the long walk down the nave on 29 April 2011, to stand at Prince William's side. The Choir sang the soaring anthem *I Was Glad*, written by Charles Hubert Hastings Parry from Psalm 122, as the bride processed slowly to the High Altar. Around the bride, her father Michael Middleton and her attendants, were almost 2,000 guests, all of whom would have been moved by her understated grace and beauty. Westminster Abbey, with its sweeping arches, the highest Gothic nave in the country, and a royal connection stretching back to the

Above: The bride's attendants, in high spirits as they arrive at the Abbey.

Left: Catherine with her father Michael Middleton, at the moment before she begins to walk slowly down the aisle of Westminster Abbey.

Right: The bride and her father, led by the Dean of Westminster and followed by Maid of Honour Pippa Middleton, the four young bridesmaids and two pageboys, process to the High Altar where Prince William is waiting with the best man Prince Harry.

Catherine's younger sister, Pippa Middleton, Maid of Honour, walked behind the bride and her father, holding the hands of the two youngest bridesmaids, three-year-old Grace van Cutsem and Eliza Lopes, also three, granddaughter of The Duchess of Cornwall. Seven-year-old Lady Louise Windsor, daughter of the Earl and Countess of Wessex and the Hon. Margarita Armstrong-Jones, eight, daughter of Viscount and Viscountess Linley, followed. Two pageboys, William Lowther-Pinkerton, ten, son of Prince William's private secretary and Tom Pettifer, the eight-year-old son of his former nanny, walked behind.

11th century, is a glorious building at any time, but on this occasion it was filled with a romance and magic that was felt by every guest.

A fresh green avenue of tall trees – field maples and hornbeams – and informal arrangements of cool white spring flowers along the nave and around the High Altar, gave a pastoral feeling, tempering the high majesty of the occasion. And as Catherine moved to take her place on Prince William's left-hand side, the best man Prince Harry turned to watch her approach. As she reached his side, her bridegroom gazed at her and whispered: 'You look beautiful'.

Speculation about how the newest member of the Royal Family should be addressed ended just before Catherine's wedding to Prince William. The Queen made her grandson and his bride the Duke and Duchess of Cambridge. She also made William Earl of Strathearn and Baron Carrickfergus, and Catherine holds the titles Countess of Strathearn and Baroness Carrickfergus.

Above: Man and wife, Catherine and William gaze steadfastly at each other as they emerge from Westminster Abbey.

Workers at the Royal School of Needlework, based at Hampton Court Palace, cut out delicate flower motifs from the lace fabrics of Catherine's wedding dress. They positioned the lace roses, thistles, daffodils and shamrocks on to the train and skirt, the bodice and sleeves, veil, and even the shoes, before stitching them on with absolute precision.

Right: Catherine waves to the excited crowds as she arrives at the Abbey.

THE WEDDING DRESS

Below: The bride and her Maid of Honour, sister Pippa, in the moments before the ceremony begins.

Right: The newly-married couple smile for the cameras and the crowds as they leave Westminster Abbey.

Speculation about Catherine's bridal gown mounted in the days before the wedding. Despite intense inquiries, its stunning secrets were not revealed until the moment the bride stepped out of her wedding car. Those gathered near the Abbey gasped at the perfect ivory lace and satin dress, elegant and modest, its decorous neckline and glorious swagged train perfectly echoing the serene nature of the bride, its shape complementing her perfect, slender figure.

The ivory and white lace and satin looked deliciously simple, but a world of craftsmanship, design, expertise and sheer genius had gone into its making by a team of needleworkers and dressmakers, led by designer Sarah Burton, of Alexander McQueen, the British fashion house.

Sarah Burton's design paid tribute to the British Arts and Crafts movement with an emphasis on fine materials and superb craftsmanship used to make the simple beautiful, often with a Romantic decorative style. On this occasion, her design involved the incorporation of appliquéd English and Chantilly lace, hand-cut and stitched on to the dress and the train. Each piece of lace was cut in the shape of a flower – the English rose, Scottish thistle, Welsh daffodil and Irish shamrock – before tiny stitches fastened them to the delicate fabric.

The skirt, of ivory and white satin gazar, evoked an opening flower, with a bodice of ivory satin finished at the back with 58 tiny satin-covered buttons. The silk tulle underskirt was trimmed with English Cluny lace. Catherine's soft, ivory silk tulle bridal veil, also decorated with hand-embroidered flowers, was held in place by a Cartier 'halo' tiara, loaned to the bride by The Queen. It was made in 1936 and bought by Her Majesty's father, then the Duke of York, for his wife, later Queen Elizabeth the Queen Mother. Some years later, the tiara was given to the then Princess Elizabeth to celebrate her 18th birthday. The bride's earrings were a wedding present from her parents, who commissioned a design based on their new family crest, incorporating diamond-set stylized oak leaves and acorns.

Left: Hand-in-hand, the new Duke and Duchess of Cambridge walk to their waiting carriage.

Below: Catherine travels in the 1902 State Landau to Buckingham Palace, for the wedding reception.

Right: Crowds roared their approval as the newly-weds kissed on the balcony of Buckingham Palace.

DUCHESS OF CAMBRIDGE

Catherine was brought up in a loving family, by parents whose own natural good manners and taste were passed on to their children. The world, watching her wedding, was impressed by the serenity and elegance, not only of the bride, but also of her mother Carole, and sister, Pippa. Michael Middleton, distinguished in his morning suit, played his part to perfection, while younger brother James showed a steady nerve, as he read the lesson from Romans 12 in a clear and expressive voice. If anyone had thought that Catherine, a commoner, was a less than worthy wife for Britain's future King, all doubts were dispelled when royalty and commoners were united, surrounded by the goodwill of the people.

Catherine's heart must have been full when, as the Duke and Duchess of Cambridge, she and her husband walked happily down the aisle, smiling and greeting their friends. If she was taken aback by the rapturous reception from the crowd of thousands waiting outside the Abbey, she recovered quickly to smile at those roaring approval. Waving gracefully, Catherine, with William at her side, was driven to Buckingham Palace in the magnificent 1902 State Landau.

Expectation was high from crowds waiting in front of the Palace for the traditional appearance on the balcony. What everyone waited to see was that very public kiss between the bride and bridegroom. At last the doors opened and the newly-weds emerged, hand-in-hand. Soon they were joined by The Queen and the Duke of Edinburgh, Prince Charles, the Prince of Wales and the Duchess of Cornwall, Prince Harry, Carole and Michael Middleton, their other daughter Pippa and their son James, and the young bridesmaids and pageboys.

Then it came. Not a long, lingering kiss, but not a perfunctory peck either. The crowd roared, hoping for another. The second kiss, when it came, was just that little bit more certain and won the same approval from the jubilant public. And, after a magnificent and ear-splitting fly-past by the Lancaster, Spitfire and Hurricane of the Battle of Britain Memorial Flight, it was all over, for the public at least. The Queen's reception for 650 wedding guests featured Cornish crab salad and duck terrine, smoked salmon on beetroot blinis, quail eggs and asparagus spears, langoustines, pork belly and wedding cake, with champagne to drink. The partying went on at the Palace well into the night as Prince Charles hosted a celebratory dinner and dance.

The royal couple returned to Clarence House between the afternoon and evening receptions – the Prince driving Catherine there in his father's 41-year-old open-topped Aston Martin decorated with 'L' plates, balloons and ribbon and a rear number plate that read 'JU5T WED'.

CATHERINE'S *Style*

When the nervous Catherine Middleton stood shyly with her fiancé in the grand Entrée Room at St James's Palace, to announce their engagement, she was perfectly dressed for the occasion. Her blue silk-jersey wrap dress by Issa sold out of up-market High Street stores within hours. Catherine had become a style icon overnight.

Catherine, tall and willowy, with a flawless complexion and hair that must be the envy of women everywhere, is a stylist's dream – yet, for the most part, she chooses her clothes and accessories herself. Because many of the clothes she wears come from her favourite stores – Reiss, Issa, Zara, Erdem, L.K. Bennett, Hobbs and J Brand – her look is accessible and is eagerly copied by thousands of women.

At university in St Andrews, where she and Prince William fell in love, Catherine's style was simple – well-fitting jeans teamed with pretty tops and shirts, boots and sweaters. And she has taken that look forward, preferring the uncluttered, yet elegant and stylish, to the fussy and hard-to-wear. She has shown the world a new way to wear her favourite denim jeans, teaming J Brand, Goldsign and Hudson skinnies with pretty, flat shoes, a wide belt and softly feminine tops or cashmere wraps.

Above: Catherine is stunning in a demure, stone-coloured dress on her first Canadian tour.

Above: Catherine's natural beauty is perfectly set off by her emerald green outfit.

For formal wear, she chooses classic styles in single or toning colours, so that the emphasis stays on her striking figure and looks. On the royal couple's Canadian tour, Catherine delighted the country with dresses just above the knee, like the purple silk-jersey day dress with long sleeves, gathered at the waist, by Issa and a lace navy and white shift by Erdem. Her two Catherine Walker outfits – an elegant grey shirt-dress and an eye-catching scarlet coat-dress, worn with a Canadian maple leaf brooch – were stunning in their simplicity, while the hand-painted, grey-toned silk frock she chose to wear while watching polo in Los Angeles, was made by Jenny Packham.

Far left: Catherine wears a chic, red coat-dress in Calgary, on the Canadian tour in July 2011.

Centre: A crisply pleated white skirt and navy blue lace top meets the approval of crowds at Los Angeles, California on the final day of the tour to the USA.

Left: The Duchess of Cambridge arrives at Calgary Airport looking fresh and relaxed in an elegant shirt-dress.

In her university days Catherine could be seen wearing oversize shoulder bags, but now she has replaced these holdalls by a series of coordinating clutch bags, chosen to blend with or match her outfit. Her jewellery is not ornate, rather discreet and chosen to complement an outfit – a thin gold or silver chain with a pendant and small drop or stud earrings. Her shoes, too, are stylish and simple: high-heeled courts, plain wedges or ballet-flats from L.K. Bennett, Rupert Sanderson, Prada and Tabitha Simmons are Catherine's style, elegantly completing her look.

Prince William first took special notice of Catherine Middleton when she appeared in a revealing dress at a charity fashion show, in their first year together at St Andrews University, Scotland. Like all the other students she normally dressed casually, in jeans, shirts and sweaters, wearing boots or loafers.

Her style has evolved through the couple's long courtship, taking account of the increasing public interest in her as the girlfriend of the future King. If her early outfits were not as well-chosen and coordinated as the beautiful, classical style she has quickly found, they were always tasteful and effortlessly classy.

Perhaps her heavily patterned black and white skirt did not team quite perfectly with the cream jacket and top she chose for the wedding, in 2005, of Rose Astor and Hugh van Cutsem in Burford Parish Church, but her trim figure and stylish good looks won the day. By the time Nicholas van Cutsem, Hugh's brother, married Alice Hadden-Paton at the Guards Chapel, Wellington Barracks, London in 2009, she had it exactly right with a cleverly patterned mid-blue coat-dress with a cream under-dress, a trademark clutch bag and a perfectly toning hat. She has refined her look even more, choosing deceptively simple styles that enhance her natural beauty.

Above left: Catherine attends the wedding of Hugh van Cutsem and Rose Astor at Burford in June 2005.

Left: An elegant coat-dress is worn by Catherine for the wedding of friends in August 2009.

Catherine clearly enjoys wearing hats – and looks good in all of them, from the cowboy stetson she sported in Calgary, Canada, to the stylish creations of Rachel Trevor-Morgan, The Queen's milliner. She often buys hats off the peg and will have them customized with a bow or a flower, but always with one aim in mind – ensuring that they do not dominate but rather, frame her face.

26

FROM CASUAL TO CLASSIC

Right: Chic and stylish at Cheltenham Festival, March 2007.

Far right: The Duchess chooses a military theme for her visit to Birmingham, in August 2011.

Right: Catherine looks sophisticated in a stunning hat, at the wedding of The Queen's granddaughter Zara Phillips and rugby player Mike Tindall, in July 2011.

Far right: A classic, sporty look for Catherine, on the tour of Canada in July 2011.

From girl-about-town before her marriage, to well-groomed Duchess attending formal occasions, Catherine has succeeded in getting her fashion look right every time. Since their marriage she and William have been socializing with the rich and the famous, from Michele Obama to Nicole Kidman, and the Duchess, with winning simplicity, has looked perfect for every occasion. Her secret? She has a natural, intuitive sense of style, knowing instinctively what suits her and how to wear it. She likes elegant, timeless dresses, often with fitted waists that emphasize her perfect figure and long legs.

When it comes to evening-wear, Catherine often chooses muted colours, pearl greys, soft lilacs or plain cream, such as the ivory gown she wore for her wedding party and the floating, gathered lilac evening dress – both by Sarah Burton at Alexander McQueen – that she sparkled in at the Hollywood BAFTA 'Brits to Watch' party in 2011. She also looked simply stunning at the ARK children's charity gala at Kensington Palace, in a breathtaking gown of palest pink tulle, encrusted with crystals, made by Jenny Packham.

Before her marriage, she was to be seen with Prince William at weddings of their friends, when she teamed dresses in her favourite deep blues and, sometimes, red, with flattering hats and pinch-waisted jackets. At formal occasions, such as when Catherine was invited by the Royal Family to watch Prince William become a Knight of the Garter, or when he passed out of the Royal Military Academy at Sandhurst, she dressed in classic tailoring, in bright colours.

Above: Dressed to perfection, Catherine wears an ivory silk gown and angora shrug, for the evening celebrations following her marriage to Prince William.

Right: The Duke and Duchess attend a charity gala dinner at Kensington Palace in June 2011. Catherine wears a pale pink tulle gown embellished with crystals.

Right: A deceptively simple, flowing lilac gown is Catherine's choice for the BAFTA 'Brits to Watch' event in Los Angeles.

Catherine
& 'THE FIRM'

By December 2006, Catherine was already receiving coaching from Buckingham Palace aides on how to cope with the intense media attention that came her way. She had the support of the Prince's press team and, when she was with William, her own protection officer. Nobody knew if William had asked her to be his wife, but the Palace was taking no chances; she was treated as one of 'The Firm' – the Duke of Edinburgh's semi-serious name for senior members of the Royal Family. By the time she and Prince William were married, Catherine had become adept at dealing politely but firmly with intrusive questions, requests for interviews and photographs.

Both Catherine and William applaud the invaluable work done by many charities, and while the Prince is already deeply involved in fund-raising for good causes, his wife is exploring her options in that direction. St James's Palace has confirmed that she will continue meeting people and making visits to charities, to evaluate where she can help. She and Prince William visited a charity for the homeless in downtown Los Angeles on their visit to America in the summer of 2011, and she was an honoured guest at a children's charity gala at Kensington Palace in June that year.

Meanwhile, she is already supporting her husband and his family in boosting morale for British enterprise, business and the community, both at home and abroad. While Prince William has undertaken such duties since his childhood, Catherine, although new to the job, is approaching it with a maturity and confidence that is already winning public hearts.

As she and William undertook their first public engagement together, on a chilly February day in Trearddur Bay, near their home in Anglesey, North Wales, Catherine, wearing a chocolate-trimmed camel coat, cracked a bottle of champagne on the bows of a new inflatable boat at the RNLI station. Later, they were welcome guests at their old university St Andrews, where they launched the institution's 600th anniversary celebrations.

Left: Catherine successfully launches a new lifeboat in Trearddur, Wales in February 2011.

Above: Catherine meeting the public at a visit to St Andrews, Scotland in February 2011.

Above: Catherine enjoys trying her hand at tossing pancakes, during a visit to Northern Ireland in March 2011.

Above: The Duchess of Cambridge shares a smile and a word with a young girl in Calgary, Canada.

In March, Catherine proved her skills at pancake-tossing on a surprise visit to Belfast on Shrove Tuesday. But it was on the royal couple's official visit to Canada, where they joined hundreds of thousands of people celebrating Canada Day, that Catherine triumphed. Smiling, relaxed and charming, she thrilled and inspired a nation, meeting and talking to sick children and cancer patients, enjoying a rock concert and watching cowboys perform at the annual Calgary Stampede.

THE *Future*
WITH WILLIAM

Catherine's husband, Britain's future King, is a working Search and Rescue pilot at RAF Valley, in Anglesey. Flight Lieutenant William Wales works with C Flight, 22 Squadron, flying Sea King helicopters. Catherine, Duchess of Cambridge is not, of course, an average RAF wife, although she and William do enjoy a happy domestic life at their rented, white-washed farmhouse, hidden away down a long and winding lane, with wonderful views over Snowdonia and a private beach. Much of their time is taken up with official duties, but on working days William leaves home early in the morning to undertake his flying duties, while Catherine looks after the house, goes shopping and prepares their evening meal. She, like William, enjoys simple pleasures – socializing with friends, sometimes driving to the local pub for supper or spending the evening at the cinema. She has always been sporty and keeps fit in the gym, or by running or taking a walk along the beach.

In London, Catherine's base is at Kensington Palace, and she and William accept invitations to Royal Family gatherings in Scotland, Norfolk and at Highgrove, the Gloucestershire home of William's father, the Prince of Wales. Catherine's family will always be of the utmost importance to her; she is close to her mother and sister, and values their company and advice. William, too, has grown very fond of the Middletons who, in turn, regard him as a son.

It is impossible for anyone to tell what the future holds, although it is as certain as anything can be that Catherine, the beautiful young woman who won the heart of a Prince, will one day become Queen Consort, offering her husband the love, help and support that he will need when it is his turn to be crowned King of Great Britain. Until that day comes, Catherine will become increasingly involved with her work for charity, using her warmth and spontaneity to encourage support for those who need it. Her natural charm brings a common touch to the modern-day Royal Family in connecting with people from all walks of life.

Left: Catherine and William, the Duke and Duchess of Cambridge, a happy team as they carry out engagements together.